To Uncle Doug
with lots of love
Graham Linda
Tony Lida and
Sarah
x x x x x

£2.50

17 DEC

The Character of Cricket

Tim Heald

THE CHARACTER OF CRICKET

Illustrated by Paul Cox

PAVILION
MICHAEL JOSEPH

First published in Great Britain in 1986 by
Pavilion Books Limited
196 Shaftesbury Avenue, London WC2H 8JL
in association with Michael Joseph Limited
44 Bedford Square, London WC1B 3DP

Heald, Tim
    The character of cricket.
    1. Cricket——England
    I. Title
    796.35′863′0942   GV928.G7

ISBN 1-85145-011-4

Designed by Lawrence Edwards

Printed and bound in Great Britain by Butler & Tanner Limited,
Frome, Somerset

CONTENTS

Introduction   7

Chelmsford   10

The Parks   18

Trent Bridge   24

Hove   34

St Helen's, Swansea   44

Edgbaston   54

The Sixth Form Ground, Harrow   62

Horris Hill   70

Bristol   76

Old Trafford   84

Northampton   92

Arundel   100

Grace Road, Leicester   108

Torry Hill   118

Ramsbottom   120

New Road, Worcester   126

Headingley   132

The Racecourse Ground, Derby   140

The St Lawrence Ground, Canterbury   148

Cannonball Cricket, Hounslow   154

Taunton   160

The Oval   168

Jesmond   176

Southampton   180

Trantridge Hardy   188

Lord's   196

I once met a man who saw Bradman batting at Moose Jaw. He remembered little about it except that it was a great event in the life of that small Saskatchewan prairie town and also an incongruous one. Bradman sparkled briefly and got himself out. There was a large crowd. End of story.

The idea of *cricket* in Moose Jaw is so very odd. Could it be a place where the Don would be appreciated? Could there be a pavilion and flags and a wrought iron weathervane incorporating stumps and a figure of Father Time ... umpires in long white coats ... scorers with sharpened HB4s and mystic erasers ... a pub ... a church with a tower and a clock stuck not at ten to three but nearer four ... and not Rupert Brooke's epideictic honey but cucumber or sandwich spread for tea ... and a tree, spreading or weeping about the long-on boundary ... and deck chairs ... and old vicars sleeping therein? Surely not in Moose Jaw? It is the ground as much as the game which makes cricket, and Moose Jaw, I think, is a place for a baseball diamond and pop corn and old men who spit tobacco. Cricket needs an appropriate setting as much as worship needs a good church.

I was never much of a cricketer, though I enjoyed it at prep school. That was a lovely ground: thatched pavilion and the Quantocks in the background. At public school somehow the fun seemed to go out of it. If you dropped catches it was early morning fielding practice and being shouted at. Winning mattered too much, and laughing on the field of play would have been a beatable offence if anyone had even contemplated it. After school I think I only played once, for my college social side against Great Tew, one of the most beautiful of English villages, though the ground was dull. I opened the innings and was bowled first ball. The humiliation was too much and I hung up my boots for good.

But I have always liked the idea of cricket. A day sitting in a deck chair in the sun, preferably with at least one similarly inclined companion to while away the longueurs between overs, seems to me a very civilised way of spending one's time. If the game becomes exciting, so much the better, though anyone who thinks that cricket can or should be consistently exciting fails, I think, to understand the game's appeal. It's like, to return to Moose Jaw and Canada for a moment, the train journey to Vancouver. You have to spend all that time trundling across the featureless prairies in order to appreciate fully the true excitement of the Rockies. By the same token, you don't really appreciate Botham's batting if you haven't had to sit through a fifty from Roebuck first. Whoever dreamed up the Sunday tip-and-run they call the John Player League did not understand this.

Much as I like the idea of such days in the sun, I had not, till the summer of '85, experienced nearly enough of them. As a child, Lord's with my mother and younger brother, getting a last glimpse of Denis Compton and a first of Fred Titmus; Taunton, but only once; village cricket on the recreation ground opposite Holly Cottage, Fulmer, Bucks; school cricket; very occasionally a match in which my father took part, though he was not designed for cricket, being, temperamentally at least, one of nature's baseball players.

As an undergraduate I lazed around the Parks in Oxford from time to time, watching the incomparable Pataudi and wondering how I could get out of writing that week's essay on Diggers and Levellers for Christopher Hill. And as an adult I have been a regular attender at Lord's as well as a compulsive pauser whenever I pass a game at Putney or at Kew or even further afield. I once watched Barbados at home and sat opposite Clyde Walcott at lunch.

Entering my fifth decade, I suddenly realised that when I turned to the cricket scores at the back of the daily paper, I was reading about far away places of which I knew nothing. I had never been to Trent Bridge; Old Trafford was little more than a name; Edgbaston was hardly even that. I had a picture in my mind's eye of Hove and Canterbury, of Headingley and St Helen's, but I had never been, never seen for myself. I relied for my knowledge on the writings of men like Alan Gibson or the talking of such as Brian Johnston. Professional cricket writing and talking is better than that devoted to any other game, but even so I felt I was missing out. I therefore decided that I would at least visit a championship ground in each of the first-class counties and a few others besides. I wanted to put faces to a few names.

I chose Harrow not Eton, Oxford not Cambridge, and only one perfect English village to stand for hundreds.

No one will agree with my selection, straightforward though much of it is. The genial A. S. R. 'Tony' Winlaw was a fervent advocate of two old country club grounds, one in Northamptonshire and the other in Northumberland; Dicky Rutnagur, another *Telegraph* writer, was fervent in praise of Wellingborough; my taxi driver in Swansea equally so on behalf of the Gnoll at Neath. I have disappointed them all. The same Winlaw was adamant that I should not go to Derby and he was fairly horrified to see me at Northampton. Sorry about that. I was curious. And I enjoyed both.

Statisticians and the seekers after objective truth will not approve either. This is not the sort of definitive work which lists ground capacity to the nearest buttock or tells you *exactly* how much Surrey loam goes into the wicket every year. It is a much more prejudiced and personal volume than that. In each case I wrote to someone connected with the ground – usually the county secretary. If he replied we agreed on a day that I might visit. Sometimes I was given a reading list. Sometimes some material written by the secretary himself. Most were helpful and hospitable. Only two did not answer my letters, but I went to their grounds just the same. Some days it rained; some it shone; sometimes I saw Zimbabwe; sometimes Australia; once or twice I ran into the oldest inhabitant; occasionally I came across prep school boys seeking autographs who reminded me of myself thirty years ago and more. I took against some grounds and I warmed to others. Sometimes I could identify reasons for this; as often as not, I couldn't.

More than any other game cricket is an experience. It takes so long that it could hardly be otherwise. I have tried here to capture some experiences garnered in the often damp summer of 1985, a summer which, despite the weather, contained some marvellous cricket and some close results. But I wasn't really interested in the play except as an excuse and a backdrop. This is not an anatomy of a cricket season. I was more interested in the sense of place.

Most of my grounds began their active life about a hundred years ago, and many of those charming Victorian and Edwardian stands and pavilions are crumbling away now. I cannot say that their replacements are often an improvement. I do not like plate glass or dried blood brick in a pavilion, and I do like flagpoles and belfries and wrought iron weathervanes. I am not a fan of 'the executive box', which is the single most obvious innovation on the county cricket ground, with the possible exception of its blood brother, the advertisement hoarding. I am fogeyish about 'Four 'n' Twenty Pies' and 'Castlemaine XXXX' and would prefer plain white wooden railings around the boundary. Modern first-class cricket, and some second-class cricket too, is not made possible by the paying spectators but by TV and commercial sponsors. The modern grounds reflect this.

And yet as I traipsed about the Kingdom from cricket match to cricket match I became increasingly aware that there are few better places to be on a summer's day; that the natives are friendly and the beer well kept; that the entertainment on the field is matched by the entertainment off it; and that, from Taunton to Tyneside and from Lord's to Leeds, there is still a character to cricket which is unique.

CHELMSFORD

'On the public side,
chaps had taken off
their shirts'

You can tell the way to the county ground by the bags. Sometimes they are canvas, sometimes plastic, occasionally leather, seldom string. They tend to have longish handles and are carried at the trail with the shoulder hunched so that the bottom of the bag is only a foot or so from the pavement. The bags bulge. This is hardly surprising for they contain an ample picnic lunch of sliced white bread sandwiches filled with Shippams paste or processed cheese; apples and/or chocolate bars – usually Kit-Kat – for filling in gaps; at least one extra sweater; a plastic raincoat; binoculars; a scorebook; pencils plus sharpener; and some form of statistical reference book.

The bags were much in evidence when I just caught the 10.10 from Liverpool Street one Tuesday in August. For Londoners aiming to get to Essex's county headquarters in Chelmsford for the first ball of the day, the 10.10 is the train to catch. It gets into Chelmsford, BR willing, at around twenty to eleven, which gives one ample time to follow the bag owners across the road past the Chelmer Institute of Education, right past the TA Centre (Royal Anglian Regt and Essex Yeomanry), left along the main road, then dip underneath it using the footpath which takes you over the narrow river and into the ground by the Britvic Picnic Area. Britvic, the soft drink makers, are a Chelmsford company and they have provided a rather dinky corner overlooking the river where one can sit at a picnic table and eat one's own food or the fast stuff – burgers, scampi, gammon or chicken – from the new Riverside Restaurant. Unfortunately you don't get a proper view of play from the picnic area but it's still quite appealing, and it makes up for the lack of a pub at the corner of the ground. Ideally a county ground has a pub at the corner, but Chelmsford does not.

This is probably because Chelmsford is so spanking new. For fifty years Essex played at Leyton. I love the idea of Leyton not least because it was the scene of the game's most famous batting record – the 555 that Holmes and Sutcliffe put on for the first wicket for Yorkshire against Essex in 1932. Sutcliffe made 313 and Holmes 224 not out.

Just a year later they sold Leyton. The reasons given were financial though maybe they were depressed at playing on a ground where the opponents scored 555 for the first wicket. For the next thirty years the county went walkabout. They continued to play occasional matches at Leyton and they also performed at Southend and Westcliff-on-Sea, at Ilford and Clacton and Chelmsford. In 1967 they decided they must have a permanent HQ and settled on Chelmsford where the club was originally founded at the Shire Hall in 1876.

The Chelmsford ground was played on by the Chelmsford club who have since moved on to a neighbouring park. It was quite small and had virtually no amenities. Everything at the modern ground – pavilion, T. N. Pearce Stand, terracing, executive boxes and committee room, even the much vaunted hospitality room for players' wives, girlfriends and other guests – has been added since 1967. In the last few years the club has spent more than seven hundred thousand pounds on improvements of one kind and another. For a county cricket club it is stunningly prosperous. The most recent treasurer's report says, 'A really excellent year on the playing field was more than reflected in the substantial increase of income over expenditure of 83,215 pounds.' Peter Edwards, the secretary/manager, says that their most persistent financial problem is fending off the more unreasonable demands of the Inland Revenue.

It was the last day of a championship match against Middlesex. Middlesex were leading the table and anxious for a win, but the match had been ruined by rain. Now at last the sun was shining and the sky was blue but to give anyone a chance there had to be some artificial 'sporting declarations'. The Middlesex first innings had realised 234. Essex then went in and declared at 33, whereupon Middlesex swatted around briefly before coming in with their score at 70. This left the home side to score 272 to win off 83 overs. In the top of the Pearce Stand a man in a blue sun hat pencilled the bowling figures into his scorebook and said, 'That's only 3.5 an over. I call that a very sporting declaration. Especially for Middlesex.' Then he paused. 'Well, it would be a sporting declaration if we could get Gooch back from Old Trafford. We're not biased, are we?'

The glum news from Old Trafford was that bad light and rain had prevented any play so far. Emburey and Edmonds had been slowly teasing the Australians out and, since they had a great deal of leeway to make up on the first innings, optimists had been hoping for an England win.

The pavilion at Chelmsford is an odd asymmetrical building with a mainly wooden top deck. It is at right angles to the wicket. The dressing-rooms are on the top floor, and players enter the field of play by coming down outside steps on the left of the building. I get the impression that as a general rule professional cricketers don't much like having to walk through a long room full of spectators, as they do at Lord's, especially if they have been out for nothing. At Lord's they nearly always avoid any eye contact with anyone when they pass through the pavilion. I guess that an arrangement like that at Chelmsford suits them better.

You can sense the club is thriving. Just inside the door of the pavilion they display the scorecards of the Second XI and the Under-25s, along with notices from the Essex Cricket Society and the Institute of Groundsmanship. 'Have you ever wished that the cricket season could last for ever?' asked the Essex Cricket Society, advertising its annual dinner, with Graham Wiltshire and Don Oslear as guest speakers, and a December party with free mince pies. The Institute offered professional assistance for anyone with a dodgy cricket ground: 'Does the ball either hit you on the brain, box or boots? Is the outfield a marsh or a rocky desert? Do you suffer from fusarium, thatch or moles?' If so your friendly neighbourhood groundsman would be round at once.

Most of the ground floor of the building is taken up with a long room or 'Long Room', with a bar at one end, full length windows looking out on to the pitch and rather horrible red, blue and gold overhead lights. These are the county colours, but even so.... The glass cases and pictures are here. The official line that I was given was that these are less impressive than the county would wish. This is ascribed to the newness of the ground, the disappearance of Leyton as cricket HQ and those peripatetic years wandering to and from the seaside. In fact, though the Chelmsford history section is a bit spotty and eclectic, it is a great deal more impressive than that at several more historic grounds.

Quite a lot is devoted to Morris Nichols, a right-arm fast bowler and forcing left-hand bat who played fourteen times for England between the wars. Nichols did the double eight times and had some stunning all-round performances. Against Gloucester in 1938 he scored 159 and took nine for 37 in the first innings and six for 128 in the second. Hammond fell to him twice. Better still was the Yorkshire match at Huddersfield in 1935. Yorkshire were champions twelve times between 1918 and 1939 and only lost forty-nine matches in all that time. The memory of that 555 opening partnership at Leyton was still fresh in the mind, but Nichols and Essex annihilated the home team. Nichols made 146 out of Essex's 334. Yorkshire scored 31 in the first innings and 99 in the second, Nichols taking four for 17 in the first and seven for 37 in the second. No wonder his blazer is in the Chelmsford pavilion.

Johnny Douglas, the county captain from 1911 to 1928, is the other most memorialised player in the Long Room, but Essex are keen to add to their collection and anxious to hear from anyone who might have interesting items to loan or bequeath. Not everything has to do with Essex. There is a photo of the sparrow killed by a ball bowled by Jehangir Khan at T. N. Pearce at Lord's and the menu for the dinner to wish Sir Julien Cahn's XI bon voyage before they embarked on a tour of Jamaica.

The team photograph of 1896 includes the scorer, Mr Armour, wearing a bowler hat; the 1979 one shows a team which won the Benson and Hedges and the Championship. Lurking in the early ones you can find C. J. Kortright, reputed to be the fastest bowler of all time. And in another print you can see another demon Essex fast bowler, poor Kenneth Farnes. Farnes is not in flannels but in RAF

gear, having a uniform pinned to his chest. He was killed in action in 1941 and apart from Yorkshire's Hedley Verity was probably the best cricketer killed in the second war.

I love these cricket museums for their quirkiness and lack of logic. Here, as in other grounds, I felt like a man suddenly let loose on a grandmother's attic. Who was the first Englishman to score two separate hundreds in a Test? Why, Jack Russell – 140 and 111 against South Africa at Durban in 1923. And who is this distinguished clerical gentleman portrayed by 'Spy'? It is the Reverend F. H. Gillingham, who scored nineteen hundreds for Essex and took 201 off Middlesex at Lord's in 1904.

And talking of clergymen, I found a real live cricket-watching parson, almost the last of the breed, sitting at a table in the Long Room watching intently as McEwan savaged the Middlesex bowling. Yet more improbably, he was wearing a straw boater. 'You can raise it to the ladies,' he explained, when I questioned him on the hat, 'and it's a wonderful shade, because I've only got the sight in one eye.' This turned out to be Major the Reverend Philip Wright, a lifelong Essex supporter, twenty-two years with the Army as a chaplain, sometime parson of Roxwell and of Woodford, whence he would bicycle to see the county play at Leyton and at Ilford. A country boy from Suffolk, he is an author too: *Traction Engines, Old Farm Implements, Old Farm Tractors, Salute the Carthorse, Country Padre, Day after Day,*

Rustic Rhymes.... For years he has been the commentator at the annual parade of shire horses in London. A year before this day at Chelmsford he had gone down with cancer and pneumonia. The doctor told him he'd have to have major surgery and Major the Reverend Wright said that he'd had a pretty good life so far and he didn't know that he could be bothered with major surgery and he'd rather just shuffle off if it was all the same to the doctor. Whereupon a young sister, Sister Sumner, formed up at his bed side and said that he hoped he wouldn't mind her being ever so presumptuous but he was old enough to be her father and if he were her father she'd want him to have the operation so he would be around for a few more years yet. So the Reverend Major thought some more and told the doctor he would have the operation after all. 'I was prayed for by the Anglicans,' he says, 'and by the Roman Catholics and by the good old Salvation Army. And here I am, and I thank God for being alive.'

Out in the middle Pringle was batting. Philip Wright was a fan of Pringle's, always had been ever since he had heard his coach at Felsted School singing his praises. The chairman's report had a rather startling line about Pringle. After complimenting him on his form, it continued: 'It is infuriating to hear occasional loud, uninformed and ill-mannered criticism of him from a small section of the members.' When I asked the padre about this he said, 'They thought he got into the England team too soon. And he wore a ring in one ear.'

It was the first time all season that I'd smelt sun tan oil on a cricket ground. Not, of course, in the inevitable sponsors' executive boxes and tents. (Cundell Corrugated were the match sponsors.) But on the public side, over by the old hospital now up for sale, chaps had taken off their shirts. The wicket was well on their side of the square and they had a closer view than my reverend friend in the boater. 'Jardine's Insurance Knows no Boundaries.' 'Bolingbroke and Wenley – Chelmsford's Department Store.'

It must be a grand place that has a department store called 'Bolingbroke and Wenley', and so it is. Wandering lonely by the main gate I asked a gateman if the stands and floodlights just outside were the home of Chelmsford Town Football Club. 'Town?' he repeated, scandalised. 'Town!? We've got a cathedral! It's Chelmsford *City*.' Indeed the ground felt like a City Ground, with its grandstands each side. It could accommodate twelve thousand, but they're lucky to get twelve hundred. The last big crowd was in the late sixties, when they drew Ipswich in the FA Cup. Their fixture list reveals Aylesbury United and Basingstoke United, Corby, Folkestone and King's Lynn. These days it is the cricket that prospers in Chelmsford.

Peter Edwards, watching play from behind his huge plate windows, ticked off evidence of this prosperity. His must be the grandest secretary's office in county cricket. It used to be the committee room, and it's big and full of trophies. He waved expansively at the ninety-four advertising boards; drew my attention to the fourteen consecutive years in profit and to the eight thousand members; to the £101,000 taken at the gate (almost four times as much as Notts, he told me). Once or twice we were interrupted. There was an ugly moment when Brian Hardie was hit on the helmet by a ball from Cowans. Down he went, to be helped off groggily and sent to hospital. Later Mr Edwards paused to deliver a public address or two from the mike. During one of these interludes I noticed a model microphone. It had been presented to commemorate the 1983 championship and was a model of the very microphone that Dame Nellie Melba had used in her great pioneering song broadcast put out by Marconi of Chelmsford in 1920. I had never known about that. Above the model, by way of proof, was a photograph of the Dame looking very glamorous in a hat.

The clouds began to bank ominously that afternoon but McEwan made a hundred, duly acknowledged by the secretary on his microphone – so much more effective than Melba's. Then Pringle, apparently not wearing his ear-ring, took up the challenge, and saw them home. The Reverend Major and the Secretary were suitably pleased and I had a pint of Tolly Original bitter, the local bitter. Then I cut through the 'city' centre on my way back to the Liverpool Street train. I have to say I was not convinced.

The great statue to Chelmsford's greatest son spoke of his serene wisdom and purest love of justice and unwearied kindness and predicted that he 'will be held by his country in undying remembrance'. Alas this Lord Chief Justice does not even feature in my biographical dictionary. And the cathedral, which looked much more like a parish church than a cathedral, was closed. No self-respecting cathedral should close at six.

But the Essex club and ground *are* impressive. 'Six championships in six years', wrote Tom Pearce, their president and former skipper, in his preface to the Yearbook. They win on the field more often than not these days and this success is complemented off it. If I have a serious complaint about the county ground, it is their lack of gates. They have no grand wrought-iron entrance. This is, however, being remedied. The members are subscribing and Mr Edwards says that they will be in place soon. At the moment they are to be called 'The Members' Gates', but the Essex buzz is that they will be named 'The Fletcher Gates'. It would be a suitable tribute to Captain Keith OBE, twenty-three years an Essex player, twelve their skipper and the man who took them to their first ever championship.

To be honest, though, I would rather they were named after an old and faithful supporter, the author of *Salute the Carthorse* and *Country Padre*. I shall always associate Chelmsford Cricket Ground with the parson in the boater. I don't suppose 'The Wright Gates' will ever happen, but I like the idea of a wrought-iron tribute to Major the Reverend Philip.

THE PARKS

'Misuse or removal of or damage to University property is prohibited. This includes picking flowers'

I had forgotten what a bossy old autocrat the University of Oxford is in its own back yard. The notice by the gate says, forbiddingly, 'This is University Property. All persons who enter and remain in the Parks do so subject to the following rules.' The rules are the usual sort of small print about the closing time, and no litter and no bikes and no loudspeakers. Mention is made of a fearsome sounding figure called 'The Parks Constable', and there is a wonderful catch-all phrase which warns you that 'Misuse or removal of or damage to University property is prohibited. This includes picking flowers.' I see the point, but it's a singularly unromantic one. The Oxford Parks are exactly the sort of place where a young man should feel obliged to pick a flower for a girlfriend as they wander towards the banks of the Cherwell. The Parks are very beautiful in the best English tradition of open countryside tamed and cultivated: half-way between meadow and garden.

Perhaps the oddest note on the board by the gate is the one which says, 'The use of the pitches for organised games without the consent of the curator is prohibited.' This, after all, is a home of first-class cricket and has been since 1881. Yet, if the University XI wants to play a single match after the end of term, Dr Simon Porter, the club's senior treasurer and fixture secretary, must make a formal application in writing. Once term is ended and the truncated cricket season concluded in mid-June, the ground is turned over for dons' tennis courts. Oxfordshire would dearly love to play on this, possibly the most beautiful of all English grounds, but the dons' tennis takes precedence.

It was looking just as it should last May – banks of sprouting pale green leaf and sharp, bright pink and white cherry blossom shielding Norham Gardens and Lady Margaret Hall to the north, the funny soaring brick Gothick of Keble Chapel to the south-east: an idyllic landscaped setting with only a few assorted horrid modern science laboratory blocks in the distance to remind you that there is another world out there. There should have been old men dozing fitfully in the ancient deck chairs, girls in summer frocks lying on the grass and making daisy chains.

No such luck. A day which had dawned sunny in London had become grey and almost foggy as I drove over Christmas Common, and Oxford was damply raw despite the lilac and laburnum. I counted seven stalwarts watching the cricket at the day's beginning. The cricketers themselves were sweatered and shivering.

The university was playing Hampshire and performing respectably. Three of their best players were away taking their Final Exams but the team had scored 303 for eight declared in the first innings. People tend to ignore performances like this, concentrating instead on the

dismal day earlier in May when Oxford accumulated only 24 in their
first innings against Leicester. Dr Porter, a former Blue himself as well
as vice-captain of Oxfordshire and captain of Headington, was rather
miffed that John Woodcock had been given front page space in *The
Times* to draw attention to the debacle. Woodcock, editor of *Wisden*,
had not been at the game, and conditions had been dreadful because
moisture had got under the covers, making the wicket virtually un-
playable. Dr Porter said any side would have had trouble on it.

All the same Woodcock made some fair points. More than four
thousand of those technically eligible to play for the university are
now women, and for some unfathomable biological reason women
can't play cricket as well as men. Dr Porter, who has a PhD and is
plainly no academic slouch, also echoed the popular sportsman's complaint about too much emphasis on intellectual achievement. I mentioned that I had been up with the younger Pataudi and remembered
a wonderful fifty he made in the Parks, putting Frank Worrell's West
Indians to the sword in 1963. Pataudi, no scholar at Winchester, had
scraped a fourth in Oriental Languages. 'Precisely,' said Dr Porter,
'and look what Pataudi did for the University. Same with Imran Khan.'
He didn't want to follow the American pattern and admit 'students'
on sports scholarships, but he didn't see why dons should positively
discriminate against games-playing candidates who have the necessary
academic qualifications. 'They do that?' I asked naively. 'Oh, yes,' he
said. Even the geography faculty, a traditional refuge for the aspiring
Blue, has tightened up. Cambridge are luckier. They have something
called 'Land Economy'. 'I like the idea of a man working for a degree
and playing first-class cricket,' said Dr Porter combatively as he stared
out of the pavilion window into the mist. 'What better training for
life?'

It's a jolly little pavilion: high gabled Victorian with one big room,
much beamed, where the players have their lunch. That day the Hampshire men in tracksuits were sitting about playing dominoes. The tables
were laid, half-pint bottles of beer in little clusters of four. There was
one wife or girlfriend present in a jump suit with leg warmers. The
professionals seemed mildly, though not aggressively, bored.

All around this room are boards with the names of all the Oxford
cricket Blues year by year from 1827. Ted Wilson, the assistant secretary, pointed out curiosities and celebrities. 'There's Bosanquet – Reg-
gie's father, who invented the googly. And C.B. Fry. And see here –
R.P. Moulding. You may not have heard of him but he got more Blues
than anyone.' I hadn't heard of Moulding, but there he is on no less
than six separate boards from the late seventies to the early eighties.
Moulding got past those perverse examiners without any trouble.
Moulding got a first. There are many Mouldings on the boards, men
whose finest cricketing hours were here playing for the University but
who scarcely troubled the scorers subsequently. But there are some of

the greatest names in cricket too: Cowdrey (he went down without taking a degree and I doubt whether the authorities would look too kindly on him if he had been born thirty years or so later than he was); Dexter; both Pataudis; M. J. K. Smith, now president of the club. Some names have odd associations for me – A. L. Dowding, captain in '53, a Rhodes scholar. Dowding once occupied my room in Balliol. 'Ah, Mr Dowding,' my scout used to recall. 'He was a real gentleman.' M. M. Walford, 'Oh, Lor' Micky' we called him at Sherborne. He was housemaster of Abbey House and used to score hundreds for Somerset in the summer holidays. And there are more recent Blues like Imran and Tavaré still in county cricket. Of this year's maligned team several are on first-class county books. Carr has signed for Middlesex; Thorn for Warwickshire. Oxford is still, against the odds, a genuine nursery of the game.

Upstairs, usually locked and seldom used, there is another small room full of dusty mementoes. One of the Hampshire team, suffering from 'flu, was lying prostrate on the window seat. A signed portrait of W. G. Grace hangs on one wall, and stacked above a cupboard are the old scorebooks. Ted Wilson pulled one down at random. 'Bit of history, eh?' he said. It was 1884. University versus the Australians. Spofforth and Bannerman were in the side. A little later we found the 1905 Australian game. The Aussies won. Trumper made 77, but the undergraduates weren't disgraced. The Hon. L. N. Bruce made 69 in the first innings. I bet he wouldn't get past the examiners these days. 'It's not a complete set,' said Wilson. 'The pavilion was commandeered by the Army during the war and they burned some of them to keep warm. I suppose they had other things on their minds apart from cricket.'

The person I felt most sorry for was Ken Tichbon of the Oxford Travel Agency. At least Ted Wilson, in his tiny office, had a single-bar electric fire. Ken Tichbon was under canvas, with only alcohol to warm the inner man. Mr Tichbon's tent – a big tent but not quite grand enough to be described as a marquee – was the first place I visited. The notice at the entrance said the public weren't allowed in unless invited, but I poked my head through the opening and was immediately asked to have a drink by the convivial and affable Mr Tichbon, who was sporting two weeks' worth of Cypriot sun tan and a Hampshire Cricket Club sweater.

He is a life-long Hampshire supporter and likes to sponsor their match against the University. For a few hundred pounds he enjoys the privilege of entertaining friends and business contacts at the ground. He regards it as money well spent, a perfect way of combining business with pleasure. All told, such sponsorship brings in over £3,000 a year – a useful addition to the annual grant from the TCCB.

Mr Tichbon was doing things in style. There was champagne cooling in Ted Wilson's fridge (though it hardly needed it) and the catering was being done by Merton College – the best, according to him, in town. Cold beef, cold salmon, cold turkey, cold ham; salads, stilton. All delicious. We were a rather motley assortment. The airlines were represented by Olympic and Air Canada; the banks by the manager of Lloyds; All Souls by their butler, who looked in for a jar and a beef roll around tea-time. He had some jolly tales of the day Russell Harty came to the college to see A. L. Rowse. Tony Winlaw, better known to *Telegraph* readers as A. S. R. Winlaw, produced some amazingly esoteric pieces of knowledge. He could reel off the names of every single first-class county captain of 1946 – a matchless party trick – but I did manage to surprise him by guessing that Ken Farnes was one of only two fast bowlers feared by Len Hutton. He then capped this with a blow by blow account of Farnes's performance for the Gentlemen against the Players in 1937.

Very, very occasionally during the afternoon the crowd swelled to double figures. Over towards Keble two boys threw a boomerang. Down by the Cherwell a stout lady in lisle stockings shouted at her King Charles spaniel. She looked like a lecturer in medieval history, an authority on Beowulf and Bede. A black labrador strayed on to the pitch and no one cared. A Brideshead male blond sat briefly on a bench, college scarf muffling his chin, *Times* sticking from tweed jacket pocket. From inside Ken Tichbon's tent came the hum of contented chat, though no one looked out to watch the cricket moving to its placid, inconclusive end.

All round the prettiest ground in England the blossom blossomed and the light grew steadily worse.

TRENT BRIDGE

*'Larwood's delivery
was too fast
to detect with
the naked eye'*

The first thing a post-war cricket lover asks an old Trent Bridge hand is 'Was Larwood as fast as they say?' At least to me, whose earliest live fast bowlers were Statham and Trueman, that seemed the obvious opening question for Harry Dalling who, according to local folk-lore, was born in the pavilion at Trent Bridge in 1921 and has lived there ever since. (Local folklore is, as usual, slightly misinformed, but more of that later.)

We were sitting behind the wicket at the bowler's end in the room from which Mr Dalling makes announcements over the Tannoy. ('Will the owner of a blue Vauxhall, registration number. . . .')

'He used to bowl from the Radcliffe Road End,' said Mr Dalling, thoughtfully, gazing down at the broad lawn where a distinctly quick Richard Hadlee was trying to blast out a Leicester eleven depleted by England calls on David Gower and Peter Willey, 'and my father used to say to me, "If you can't see the ball, watch the batsman's pads".' More often than not Larwood's delivery was too fast to detect with the naked eye from the boundary, but if you watched the pads you would catch a glimpse of red leather as it flew past or thudded against them, causing a puff of newly applied blanco. Larwood took 1,247 wickets for Nottingham. Voce from the other end took 1,312. Fewer people remember another devastating fast bowler who played for Notts. In 1959 Keith Miller played against Cambridge University, made 164 runs and took two for 35. Henry Blofeld of the BBC opened for Cambridge. It was Miller's only match for the county and Harry Dalling was there, just as he has always been when there is play at Trent Bridge.

The ground is just south of the Trent in a part of the city given over almost exclusively to sport. It was a sad sign of the times that when I asked the taxi driver to take us to 'the ground' he dropped my son and myself outside the main gates of Nottingham Forest. It didn't much matter. The two grounds are very close, close enough for Forest to hire out their director's boxes to Trent Bridge ticket holders on big match days. All they have to do is cross the Radcliffe Road at lunch-time. The other Nottingham soccer club now lives just north of the river, but in the old days both Forest and County played at Trent Bridge. In 1897 there was an international soccer match there with England playing Ireland. In 1910 County departed, floating their old stand across the Trent to their new home. The last League match at Trent Bridge was in 1910 when County played Aston Villa.

Before the Great War you might have expected the driver of the hansom you hired at the LMS station to be a little confused about who played where, but all three grounds are quite distinct now. Forest's, however, is much the most ostentatious, with a colossal new

stand in which the red-and-white seats are arranged to spell out the club's name in vast letters.

We crossed the Radcliffe Road and entered by the gates to the right of the Trent Bridge Inn, just past the Larwood Lounge. A lot of litter on the ground. The flags fluttering proudly from the TBI were those of Skol and Double Diamond, though it was Nottingham and Leicester who were playing. All this summer the beer sponsors are much in evidence, especially the Australians. One unfamiliar one is Castlemaine XXXX. It is explained to me that they put XXXX because Australians do not know how to spell beer. I enjoy this joke because the Anglo-Australian rivalry is supposed to be spiky and too much of the spikiness has been Australian.

In the very old days the TBI used to be the Trent Bridge pavilion but that was long ago and the pub seems to have curiously little connection with the modern ground. It's like a fern bar inside, with low lights and greenery, moussaka, and wine by the glass. If you want to go for a meal you have to get an exeat from the man on the gate and go round to the front; there is no way in directly from the ground. The clientele appear to be office not cricketing folk.

I took Alexander, who was thirteen at the time, because I had always felt that Trent Bridge was a small boy's ground, a view confirmed by Cardus who called it 'the schoolboys' happy hunting ground'. In his day a boy could get a good seat for sixpence. Fifty years on it's a pound, which still seems good value, not least because there is a wide expanse of grass near the single net at the side of the ground and on the day we were there a robust pick-up game was in progress. It's just as it was in Cardus's time, when they played Nottinghamshire against Lancashire in miniature – 'the smallest boy Larwood. And as they do so they can keep their eyes on the real Larwood, and "monkey" his actions from the life.' As we watched it was Derek Randall they aped.

Michael Jayston, the actor, remembers how, as a boy, he bowled to an elderly George Gunn in the nets. In half an hour Gunn only missed one ball – but then he was using a walking stick for a bat.

It is less of a small boy's ground these days, just as most of life is less generous to small boys. At one point, when I was off searching for the elusive Harry Dalling, Alexander went and sat on the grass. There should have been no problem over this, since he was well to the spectators' side of the boundary. Needless to say, however, the inevitable officious official was soon on the spot, ordering him back into the stand. There was a reason for this of course: Alexander was dangerously close to the board which said 'Andrews Cleaning Equipment'. Had he prevented the several hundred spectators from having an uninterrupted view of their sign, Andrews Cleaning Equipment might possibly have withdrawn their support. In modern county cricket there are too many times when sponsors and advertisers take precedence over small boys.

Nottingham against Leicester is a local Derby – or would be if it was Forest against City. But it was a spotty little third-day crowd, which was a pity because Randall started the day on thirty and went on to make a century. Early on, against speed, he once did a wonderfully theatrical pratfall and lay motionless on the grass for several seconds before getting up and dusting himself off and doing a little jig. Born in Retford, he's an authentic local star, Derek Randall, with a sponsored car like any other sporting star. It has 'Derek Randall Drives with New Crown' written on it, and he had parked it rather antisocially beside the pavilion where it blocked several others.

When the slow bowlers came on he got a bit bogged down, to the evident disgust of a trio behind me in the stand opposite the car park who looked as if they were understudying for the three in *Last of the Summer Wine*. 'Only way he's going to get runs is if he moves his feet,' said one of them, an elderly black man with a thick Nottingham accent. 'Like Johnson.' And they all nodded sagely as Johnson scampered down the wicket in a charge on the spinners, while the Retford imp played as if his back foot had been cemented to the wicket. Still, he got his hundred and wasn't out, which left him top of the first-class averages by a street.

It was the librarian, Peter Wynne-Thomas, who first told me about Harry Dalling. Mr Wynne-Thomas is the author of a useful slim volume called *Cricket Grounds of Nottinghamshire*, and much else besides. When I saw him his mind was full of his new biography of Arthur Shrewsbury, W. G. Grace's favourite, but when I explained that I was looking for an authentic old Trent Bridge hand he had no hesitation. 'Harry Dalling,' he said. 'Well, he was born and bred on the premises, wasn't he?'

There were other candidates. A couple of men who came along for every match and filled in their scorebooks ball by ball; Reg Simpson, who often dropped in from the Gunn and Moore bat factory where he was managing director. Not as many ex-players hung around the way they used to, in Mr Wynne-Thomas's opinion. He remembered the Gunn brothers sitting in the same chairs match after match arguing happily way into retirement. His own observations led him to conclude that once a modern player finished he was no longer interested in watching his successors.

My search for Harry Dalling provoked much hilarity. He has an office but is seldom in it. Every time I asked one of the attendants or gate-keepers, whose boss Mr Dalling is, they would grin and say they'd been talking to Mr Dalling just ten minutes ago and he went thataway. Advised to check in at the office and shop just inside the main gates, I was met with similar merriment and comparisons between Mr Dalling and the needle in the haystack. Eventually a consensus emerged that he would be in the public address office in the pavilion. To reach this you have to climb to the top of the building where there is a sort of 'executive' dining area behind ugly plate glass. Marvellous view from within, a hideous excrescence from without, it has the unmistakable whiff of sponsor and expense account which have become, for better or for worse, so much a part of the modern game.

After running the gauntlet of the late lunchers, I was out into the open and on to an iron fire-escape-style staircase and down to a passage running the length of the pavilion. A series of glass-fronted rooms lead off this. The scorers sat in one and said that Mr Dalling would be along at the end – but the room was empty. I kept trying until one of the stewards took pity on me and said that when he finally showed up they would page me on the Tannoy. So I wandered off to the Radcliffe Road end, noticing with pleasure that a member in front of the pavilion was actually wearing a knotted handkerchief. I could not remember the last time I had seen anyone in a knotted handkerchief, let alone sitting in front of a long room. At Lord's no one in the pavilion would be seen dead with anything but a Panama on his head.

The Radcliffe Road Stand is the noisy bit where the barrackers sit – Trent Bridge's Kop, though such things are relative. Most of the

onlookers were of pensionable age and their minds were not always on the cricket.

'Oo played in that shield thing before season?' one man was asking his friend.

'Oh aye,' said the other, 'Everton. They beat Liverpool. They've won nothing Liverpool. Nothing.' This was understatement coming only days after the disastrous European Cup final in Brussels. That horror seemed worlds away from the Trent.

'Ooh! LBW. Now we've got a real chance. I still think we'll win it.'

'Oh aye.'

Southerners like me find it hard to accept that anyone outside a Bill Tidy cartoon ever says 'Oh aye!' – just as northerners can't believe that real people ever say 'Gosh!' or 'I say!' or 'Super!'

Suddenly a Nottinghamshire player dropped a catch. Not a very difficult one.

'Well I'll go to bloody 'ell,' exclaimed the most vociferous of the pensioners, addressing the rest of us with an expression of incredulous disgust. ''E were fast asleep. Fast a-bloody-sleep.' And he slapped his thigh and fell to muttering.

Tempers were shortening a little at the Radcliffe Road end. Two twelve-year-olds were eating sweets and throwing the wrappers about. The man behind lent forward and said, ' 'Ey you two. Stop it or booger off somewhere else.' The two lads stopped it but boogered off a few minutes later and I boogered off with them. No message had come over the Tannoy, but I judged it time to brave the executive crow's nest and the iron staircase and look for Harry Dalling.

He was there this time, very neat in brown, and gazing out at the play from behind a microphone. No, he said, he hadn't actually been born on the ground, but very close. His father had been superintendent of the ground just as he was now. He had only ever left Trent Bridge during the war.

'When I was a boy of seven or eight years of age,' he said, 'Walter Marshall was the groundsman and he lived in the pavilion. And every year when the Marshalls went on holiday we would move into the pavilion. Mrs Turner still lived there too. Her husband was the secretary in the 1890s. I'd take Mrs Turner to St Giles's church. And in 1929 she gave me a prayer book.

'In those days at night the anglers used to come in to look for worms. You'd see their lamps all over the ground. And where the squash courts are there were chickens and apple trees.'

After he succeeded his father, Harry Dalling slept in the pavilion until 1956. He remembers taking tea with the players when Notts played Surrey in the thirties, and he remembers Bradman making a hundred and thirty-odd in the late thirties and D.R. Jardine coming down to present something or other to Larwood and Voce. He was there when they built the Parr Stand, which was supposed to be a covered stand but the roof blew off. And he told me how years ago Monday was called 'butchers' day' because butchers always had Mondays off and they used to come along to Trent Bridge every Monday; and how in the old days they used to ring two bells before an innings, whereas now it's only one. The first one was known as the 'saddling bell', presumably because it was the signal to get padded up.

Harry Dalling played a bit for the ground staff and the Second XI and was a useful leg spinner. Like most leg spinners his eyes glaze over when he talks about the almost forgotten art. He was hugely pleased that the Australians had brought one over.

He scored for a while after the war and was on duty the famous day in 1946 when Warwickshire's Eric Hollies got ten for 46 against Notts. The old scorebooks are all in the library downstairs. One oddity is that until quite recently the Trent Bridge Test matches were recorded in the Notts Second XI scorebooks.

It was in 1949 that he took over as ground superintendent, responsible for 'everything outside the boundary rope'. He and his father and his brother, and now his nephew who is assistant groundsman, have given years of service, but in the long history of Trent Bridge it is but an evening gone.

Mr Dalling told me the story of the origins. It all began with a publican called William Clarke who was one of the great underarm lob bowlers, probably the best in England. He played in Sherwood Forest until he began to court Mary Chapman, the landlady of the Trent Bridge Inn. After they were married Clarke fenced off the open meadows round the TBI and on 10 July 1838 T. Barker's side played W. Clarke's side on 'Clark's new ground at Trent Bridge'. Just over two years later Notts played Sussex. 'Clark,' said Mr Dalling, 'was the first Kerry Packer. He was the first man in the country to charge an admission fee.'

The remark lurked at the back of my mind all through the rest of the day as the two counties played out an inexorable draw. For all Hadlee's aggression, Nottinghamshire never looked like getting Leicestershire out; and Leicester never looked like getting the runs – certainly not without Gower. At one point in our talk Harold Dalling had been scornful of Lord's and MCC with words to the effect that the high point of their season was Eton versus Harrow. Then I read Frank Keating's obituary of Percy Fender in the *Guardian* in which he said that Fender had once overheard a President of MCC refer to him as a 'smarmy Jew-boy'. And I thought of that great Notts benefactor Sir Julien Cahn with his own ground and his own team, good enough in Harry Dalling's estimate to beat any modern county. Sir Julien left his cricket bats, over a hundred of them, to Trent Bridge. He was never persona grata at Lord's.

And then I remembered my son Alexander being removed from the grass in case he obscured the sign which said 'Andrews Cleaning

Equipment', and A. W. Carr, who was sacked by Eton and ended up at my old school, who once hit a massive six over the old secretary's office at Trent Bridge and who captained Larwood in the days when Gents and Players had separate dressing-rooms. And I thought that this ground on the Trent which symbolically divides two Englands was perhaps itself a symbol. The first ground to charge admission. The ground which spawned Larwood. The ground with the ostracised Jewish benefactor.

It's very wide, Trent Bridge. You used to be able to get 7,000 spectators on the turf. 'Whenever I go to Lord's,' says Harry Dalling, 'Lord's seems so small. Here you can run five if you hit it to the far corner.'

'Oh aye,' I thought, as I retraced my steps past the Larwood Lounge and over the Trent, and I wondered whether he had meant it literally or metaphorically. The further north I travelled in cricket, the smaller Lord's seemed to become.

HOVE

'*Deck chair and handclap
and ghosts of Ranji
and Duleep and
C.B. Fry*'

Only sixty-six and two-thirds per cent of those in the immediate vicinity of Brighton Railway Station knew there was a cricket ground in town, let alone that the Australian tourists were playing on it. That was the result of my snap poll conducted shortly after getting off the train from East Croydon. Worse still, the two-thirds who knew where the cricket ground was suggested I either went by bus (6 or 37) or on foot via the Seven Dials roundabout and Goldsmid and Davigdor Roads. I footed it up the hill and down past the Davigdor House Rest Home and the green gabled Windlesham Club (founded 1905), overtaking an Indian gentleman in grey flannels and blazer and binoculars slung about him Sam Browne style. Facades were peeling around the Brighton–Hove border, and there was a sense of cat and old landlady. I noticed the Legal and General's snazzy new glass and brick and the Doris Isaacs School of Dancing in less opulent surroundings and I almost missed the cricket ground because of that obstructive modern block of flats – Cromwell Court – which dominates the North End.

They were wrong, the sixty-six and two-thirds who knew there was a cricket ground. On leaving the station you should walk south to the sea and then west along the promenade, past the Metropole and the derelict West Pier until you arrive at a wonderfully grand statue of the old Queen herself erected by the burghers of Hove in 1897. March up Grand Avenue, Hove for about three blocks, note the Victorian vastness of the Hove Parish Church – All Saints, all locked up – and the Sussex Cricketers public house, which stands as a convivial sentry box at the entrance of the ground. You can actually walk into the bar, collect a pint and enter the ground through the beer garden. In theory, anyway.

Don't be dismayed by the sign which says 'No Dogs', nor its companion, equally discreet in gold on blue, which says, 'no cricket guaranteed'. Just carry on through the Tate Gates, erected in memory of one of Sussex's greatest opening bowlers, and you're in Sussex by the Sea, a charming oasis of deck chair and hand clap and ghosts of Ranji and Duleep and C. B. Fry, of Tony Greig and John Snow and the present Anglican Bishop of Liverpool, who played here when he was simply D. S. Sheppard.

There is a front and a back entrance to the County Ground at Hove and you must always use the front.

Because Sussex were playing the Australians the Sussex Cricketers had a large banner up advertising Fosters lager, the vin ordinaire of Australia. I turned right, past the indoor cricket school erected in memory of A. E. R. Gilligan, captain of the county in the twenties, and found a seat at the back of the stand in the south-east corner of the ground. I say 'the back', but the stand is in such a state that the very back has been cordoned off as too dangerous. Most of the concrete seems to have split. To my right was a rather splendid scoreboard-cum-clocktower, with loudspeakers sticking out of the top like a couple of dowager's ear trumpets.

You would be pushed, I think, to call it a pretty ground. To north and south it is dominated by large modern blocks of flats. These have a commanding view of play but the inhabitants of the flats were all out at work or not keen on cricket because there was no one on a balcony nor with a face pressed to the glass. The Gilligan indoor school is by no means a thing of beauty, though it is practical. There are seats on the roof, which causes a certain amount of trouble with spectators moving about behind the bowler's arm. The pavilion complex reminded me strongly of a house I once inhabited for a year in Toronto. The house had started life around the turn of the century as a modest two up, two down Colonial residence but generations of settlers had found it too small. Each one appeared to have tacked a bit on, probably with his bare hands. The pavilion at Hove is a bit like that. Somewhere lurking in there is an original building but it is so barnacled about with extra seating and what appear to be small greenhouses that it is impossible to detect. The most charming part of the ground is the North End. This is a sloping green bank with several rows of gaily striped deck chairs. You can't actually see the sea but it is a welcome reminder that it is only about three blocks away. Less enjoyable, I thought, were the hard boiled eggs. I counted half a dozen of them, very large and garish, scattered round the boundary, and manufactured, presumably from some sort of polystyrene. The clue to the eggs was in a hoarding which said 'Stonegate Country Eggs' and a small note on the scorecard which said, rather strangely, 'Please let us have your empty Stonegate Egg Packs, each one is worth 3p to Sussex.'

Sussex were batting. It was grey but warm and showed signs of lifting. Thomson, the once terrifying 'Thommo' who used to partner the fearsome Lillee, was bowling up the hill. The ground slopes quite dramatically down from the north towards the sea. From my position it looked as if Thommo was bowling in a newly permed grey wig but advancing years had certainly not slowed him to military medium. I had only been watching a few minutes when the Sussex captain, Barclay, the dominant figure in a last-wicket partnership inching slowly closer to the Australian first innings score of 321, appeared to duck straight into a Thomson ball which rose quite sharply from short of a length. There was a terrible crack of leather on bone and the wounded batsman went into a whirling dervish routine before sinking to his knees somewhere around fine leg.

The spectator on my right, middle-aged, in blazer and blue espadrilles, sucked his teeth and shook his head as the fielders gathered round.

'Part of the game innit,' said his neighbour, tweed jacketed, plastic bag of lunch at his feet.

It was all rather unexpected. The pitch had looked quite placid; Barclay was chugging away comfortably and was on 37 not out. But now here he was retiring hurt and being carted off to hospital for stitches to his mouth. 'An ordinary bouncer as opposed to a wicked one' was the *Times*'s verdict, which was rather what I thought though it all looks very different when you're sitting on a deck chair several yards on the safe side of the mid-wicket boundary.

I took advantage of the lull to go and seek out Ossie Osborne. Mr Osborne is the Honorary Librarian of the Sussex County Club and what he doesn't know about Sussex cricket is not worth knowing. A keen club cricketer in his youth, he retired when he was sixty-four, but still runs Brighton Brunswick, the local mid-week club side which plays its home games on the county ground. For fifty years he worked for Joe Lyons and his finest achievements were for them. When Lyons gave him a special anniversary dinner they quoted two of his finest hours on the anniversary menu:

'On Sunday 31 July 1927 Harold Osborne playing against a Wembley Special Constables XI took all ten wickets for 33 runs and then scored 53 not out.'

And, almost better:

'Osborne helped restore the position being last out, another Constantine victim, for 67. The West Indian fast bowler finishing with 6 for 58.'

Sixty-seven against Learie Constantine! Learie used to enjoy playing at the Lyons' ground at Sudbury. There were a hundred and twenty acres and a fine club-house. In the evening after the matches there were dances in the club-house. Very good parties.

Mr Osborne is known to everyone as Ossie. Indeed the nickname is so widely accepted that even on the Brighton Brunswick fixture card he is down as Match Manager for the game against Malden Wanderers as 'Ossie'. Despite the advancing years he is extremely perky and talks incessantly, punctuating his speech with occasional apologies for talking so much and also with frequent 'God Bless You's. I wasn't surprised to learn that latterly he was a wicket-keeper. I bet he appealed a lot.

'I'm not a reader,' he says, 'but I do like research.'

When he took the job on he became infatuated – his own word – with the archives and records in his care. In the winters he took everything home and solemnly compiled a card index system which means that now every single person who ever played for Sussex since 1790 has his own card, written out in Ossie's hand.

'I'll tell you a story,' said Ossie. 'A chap writes to me from Australia and says he wants to know more about someone who played Sheffield Shield cricket and also played for Sussex. His name was E. B. Dwyer.' At this point Ossie went to his card index and got down Dwyer's entry. It turned out that he wasn't just plain 'E.B.', he was 'J.E.B.B.P.Q.C.', full name John Elicius Benedict Bernard Placid Quirk Carrington Dwyer. A goodish bowler, Dwyer took 179 wickets for the county between 1904 and 1909, including sixteen in a single match against Middlesex at Hove in 1906.

He came to Sussex because when Pelham Warner took his MCC side to Australia Dwyer played against it for a relatively minor team and evidently impressed Plum Warner. 'Well bowled,' said Plum. 'You must come and play in England.'

Dwyer took Warner at his word and took ship to England but, of course, there was no one there to meet him, and certainly not Plum Warner. Somewhat discouraged he still managed to scrounge a game in which C. B. Fry, then Sussex captain, was playing. 'Well bowled,' said Fry, after the game. 'Come down to Sussex and we'll have a look at you.' And he had a net and became a Sussex regular.

'Now read on,' said Ossie. I read. 'J.E.B.B.P.Q.C.' was, it transpired, the great-grandson of Michael Dwyer, the Wicklow chieftain, who had led the Insurrection of 1798 and been transported to Australia. That's where all those names came from.

There was a shout from outside. Ossie turned and stared out at the arena. 'Hilditch caught by Greggy,' he said. 'He won't like that.' The Australian vice-captain had been the victim of an unlucky decision in the first innings and was taking time to get among the runs.

Ossie always takes an early lunch but he let me stay in his library while he was away. He locked me in, mind you, which was a touch unnerving as the library is in a stand which feels distinctly combustible.

It's full of history. The earliest record of cricket in the county is from 1622, when four boys were reported to the vicar of Boxgrove near Chichester for playing cricket during evening prayer time. The club was founded in 1839 in convivial circumstances (like most cricket clubs) after dinner at the Old Ship. 'Most gladly received by all the lovers of this truly English and noble game' ran the contemporary report. The annual sub was a couple of guineas, and 'The club shall engage one or more men to bowl for two or more days in the week, for practice.'

Almost as interesting – almost as interesting as the commemorative album of the Installation of H. H. Maharajah Ranjitsinhji Jam Sahib of Nawanagar on 11 March 1907 – was a letter from Neville Cardus on *Manchester Guardian* paper twenty years later. It is obviously in answer to a fan letter from young Osborne. 'Your handwriting does not reveal your name,' wrote Cardus, 'else I would address you "Dear Mr ...". Your charming letter has refreshed me. Keep up your enthusiasm for the Great Game. It is one of the country's finest possessions. Write to me as frequently as you like. With good wishes yours sincerely, Neville Cardus.'

I felt rather abashed by this, because I had recently been less than enthusiastic about a collection of Cardus which I had reviewed in *The Times*. I felt the reputation was inflated, too much of the prose too whimsically florid, and I sensed also that perhaps he wasn't altogether a very nice person. Yet here was an extraordinarily generous response to an unknown admirer. Delusions of grandeur and overwork prevent most people from answering letters nearly so enthusiastically – if at all.

I soon realised why Ossie took his lunch early. As soon as he came back the players went off for their lunch and the little library became crowded with extraordinary cricket buffs. They were all after little bits of esoterica, but the one who most intrigued me was a man of thirty-odd who came in with a large scorebook filled in with what I took to be his own handwriting. 'I've got a problem,' he said. 'I'm an over missing for this game in 1952.' And he pointed to the match in question, every single ball of it neatly filled in. So Ossie went down, rather creakily, on his hands and knees and got out the 1952 scorebooks. The cricket buff frowned and pored over the pages and tried to work out why and how such a discrepancy had arisen.

Mesmerised though he is by the records and the stories, Ossie seemed quite unmoved by the actual cricket going on outside his window. When Keppler Wessels of Australia was run out by Parker he paused for a moment and said reflectively: 'Wessels ought to know better than that. He knows Paul inside out.' This was because Wessels, a South African, used to play for Sussex. Indeed he is a sort of lineal

The Sussex Cricketer

descendant of J.E.B.B.P.Q.C. Dwyer himself. But most of the time Ossie doesn't watch. Over his shoulder I could see an Australian – Greg Ritchie, I later discovered – launching himself into a handsome attack on the Sussex bowlers.

Ossie used to watch more when his old friend Jack Hobbs was alive. Hobbs retired to Hove and had a regular seat in the pavilion, though if someone else sat in it he was too modest to complain.

'Greggy's coming tomorrow,' said Ossie, talking of Tony.

'Popular round here is he?' I asked waspishly, thinking of Packer and the Establishment view of Greig as villain.

'He is with me,' said Ossie belligerently. When Greig was in the wilderness Ossie got him to turn out for Brighton Brunswick. He still has one of Greig's bats and his old blazer which he still sometimes wears when he goes out to the middle to toss a ceremonial coin. It makes him look like a very small scarecrow, a dwarf in giant's clothing, and he has a stiff imitation Wurzel Gummidge walk to add humour to the act.

De Selincourt has a passage about the County Ground at Hove in his book *The Game of the Season*. 'The County Club,' he wrote, 'in which we all take a fierce personal pride is not an aloof place of grandeur on to whose grounds we occasionally creep to watch real class cricket and creep away again, feeling very small and foolish, to our antics on the village green. Not a bit of it. It is in a very real sense the parent club; and we go to Hove or Horsham with our heads up, at our ease and welcomed, to watch and appreciate the finer points of the great game, which are not to be seen with such frequency in our own brighter, shorter and less skilful battles.'

A man in a white floppy sun hat slept that afternoon in a deck chair on the grassy slope at the North End; and, because the sun had disposed of the grey misty morning one or two had stripped to the waist and were sitting with their feet on the bench in front. In the back garden of one of the villas to the east two elderly men and a woman sat absorbed behind a makeshift windbreak of striped canvas. 'God Bless,' said Ossie as he said good-bye, and I was reminded of another passage from de Selincourt's book:

'Unostentatiously and surely, with no high-sounding talk or pulling of long, earnest faces, something is generated which takes off from cricket to the even greater game of living and that something is the spirit of active goodwill, the finest and most precious thing in life.'

Sentimental creatures, the cricket writers of the Golden Age, and yet they had their points. And even they would have enjoyed Ritchie's century and Phillips's ninety as they set the home team more than 300 to win on the final day.

I walked back along the promenade to Brighton. Fishermen sat lugubriously by their rods, young girls soaked up a far from scorching sun in bikinis, and I bought four sticks of pink-and-white Brighton rock for my children. Behind me in the distance was a separate index card for every Sussex cricketer who ever lived, and the county was slowly fighting its way to a draw.

St Helen's, Swansea

'The scoreboard at one end still said "Opponents – Barbarians"'

I wanted to stay with Mrs Evans but the St Helen's Guest House was full. All along the Mumbles Road the 'No Vacancies' signs were up in the windows along with the net curtains and the cacti. No Vacancy at the Allanton; No Vacancy at the Oyster; No Vacancy at the Marine Vista nor the Bay View nor the Seychelle nor the Tudor Court. So I stayed in the centre of Swansea at the Dolphin, which was dull and about five times the price and in a modern shopping centre complex of concrete and dried blood brick redeemed only by an authentically pompous statue of Sir H. Hussey Vivian Bt, first Baron Swansea of Singleton, luminous green with verdegris.

Swansea is one of the two main homes of the Glamorgan County Cricket Club, otherwise known as Clwb Criced Morgannwg. The County Ground is in Cardiff but I feel Swansea is the real home. In Cardiff the rugger people turfed the cricketers off the Arms Park in 1967, breaking the tradition and the continuity. Since then Glamorgan have played their Cardiff games in Sophia Gardens. In Swansea they coexist with the rugger players just as they always have since 1921 when Glamorgan cricket first became first class.

You can't get away from rugby in South Wales any more than you can escape from the Welshness of the Welsh. My mother's maiden name is Vaughan, which suggests a smidgen of Welsh blood, but the Welsh still feel foreign to me. Charming, mind – if you meet them half way, that is – but foreign all the same.

On the Red Dragon, which is what they call the six o'clock from Paddington once it crosses the border of the Principality, there was an attractive blonde in a white dress sitting next to a man with frizzy hair. She was certainly a singer and he, I think, a conductor, and I like to believe they were on their way to an Eistedffod. North of the Severn she began to sing on the crowded train, in Welsh. Newport. Cardiff. Bridgend. Neath. Rugby towns all. 'Isn't it lovely to be back in the mountains?' asked an old woman of her dog, or maybe the rest of us, as we snaked into Swansea. Surely they couldn't play cricket *here*, I thought. As well play cricket in the Pyrenees.

I knew I was wrong, of course. I knew that Wales used to play MCC in the old, old days and that S.F. Barnes once opened the bowling for them in such a match when he was fifty-seven years old. Funny sort of Welshman. I knew from that day's paper that the national team were in the process of beating Zimbabwe in – of all places – Builth Wells, though I hadn't realised that Glamorgan players can't play for Wales. Those registered for the county are available for England instead. Hence the Welsh captain of England, Tony Lewis, who also captained Glamorgan's championship-winning side in 1969. Hence also Gilbert Parkhouse, who played for England in the fifties and opened the batting for Glamorgan in the summer and played full-back for Swansea in the winter.

Today the opposition was Leicester, whom I had already seen looking a little plain at Trent Bridge. This time they were again without Gower, on duty for the Third Test, but Willey, dropped by England, was back as their star all-rounder.

I knew about Welsh cricket because I had once interviewed the legendary Wilfred Wooller, who captained the side that won the championship in '48 and who was secretary until 1977. I checked the date of my interview and found it was 1970 – just after the Archbishop of Wales had threatened to resign his Glamorgan membership if the South African cricket tour went ahead. Mr Wooller said the Archbishop was being 'unchristian', which was a characteristic Woollerism. They still talk a lot about 'Wilf' in South Wales. He played rugby and squash for Wales and was centre-forward for Cardiff City, and he gave the impression of being permanently in search of an argument. Some people call him 'Dyed in the Wooller'.

So I knew about Welsh cricket, but I had never seen it happen. And I knew about St Helen's, the Swansea ground, partly because it is where Swansea plays its rugger, partly because it is so close to the sea, and partly because it was here that Gary Sobers once hit poor Malcolm Nash for thirty-six runs in one over.

To get to it you walk along the Mumbles road going west. Odd that 'Mumbles' seems to be almost the only word in bilingual Wales that requires no translation. Not like Neudd y Sir, which means County Hall, that massive new affair on the sea front – all concrete and smoked glass; nor Multi Storey Car Park, which is Parc Ceir Aml-Lawr. There is no Welsh translation of the 1952 Prison Act, either. You can read it at the entrance to the gaol opposite County Hall. 'It is an offence for any person,' it begins, 'to help a prisoner to escape.'

The ground itself is just after the Guild Hall, which I mistook from the distance for a power station. They were holding a degree ceremony there: scrubbed young people in gowns and mortar-boards, mums in flowered hats, dads in Sunday suits, and much photography. You can see St Helen's from afar because of the huge pylons supporting the floodlights. It was the only ground to stage a floodlit game against the Australian Rugby tourists but – oh, the shame of it – there was a power cut and the lights failed.

Just to the east of it is the Patti Pavilion, Swansea's seaside theatre. Last week it had been *A Viennese Whirl*, with Angela Jenkins and John Noble; next was to be Edmund Hockridge, star of *Carousel*. To the south is the main road (noisy) and a strip of grass separating it from the beach (sandy) and the sea (busy). On the grass are two war memorials and one to Swansea Jack, 1930–1937, 'the brave retriever who saved twenty-seven human and two canine lives, loved and

mourned by all dog lovers.' I feel I should know more about Swansea Jack.

Behind the ground the hill rises steeply and the terraces are piled one on another like the terraces of Bath, except that these houses are predominantly grey with a few flashes of bright pastel where people have painted their pebbledash and created little oases of neapolitan ice cream. It crossed my mind that Dylan Thomas came from here and that perhaps one of those houses was number 5 Cwmdonkin Drive. Then I thought that the poet was probably not a cricket man, so instead I walked round to the Members' Entrance opposite the Cricketers pub.

I was wrong, as it happens, about Dylan. When he was at school his headmaster caught him climbing over a wall and asked what he was up to. With customary frankness the boy said he was bored with class and thought he might pop down to St Helen's and watch Glamorgan at cricket.

'Dylan,' said the head, 'That is very wrong of you. Very wrong indeed.' And then as he walked away, he half turned and called out: 'I hope someone catches you.'

I was an hour or so early for the start of play and was surprised to find that a net had been erected in the centre of the field and the Glamorgan players were practising on the wicket they had used in the previous day's county match. Common practice, I was told later, especially if the players have performed badly the day before – which in this case they had.

I say 'centre' of the field, but this is inaccurate. George Clement, some time groundsman at St Helen's, said with that characteristic Welsh verbal felicity that if I were to fly up a few hundred feet and look down I would see that the ground was like 'a giant light bulb'. Norman Yardley once wrote that it was like a key-hole. The narrow, westerly end is where the rugby is played. Indeed the scoreboard at that end still said 'Opponents – Barbarians'. It is flanked on the sea side by an imposing old grandstand which, in the wake of the Bradford disaster, was having £100,000 spent on improvements to it. The pneumatic drills were going full blast before play, but the workmen promised they would stop at eleven. In any case no one sits in it during cricket unless it is impossibly hot. This seldom happens at Swansea but if it does the rugby stand is the only place with any shade. All other seats are open to the elements.

Around about the half-way line there were two gold and yellow striped tents, both for sponsors. Then came the advertising boards in a crescent and the ground starts to bulge outwards into an appropriate shape for cricket. The terracing at the Patti Pavilion end is fine for watching cricket but far too far away for rugger spectators. For big rugby games they erect a special temporary stand in front of the permanent one.

The pavilion is on the north side. A large sign says 'Swansea Cricket and Football Club', and it is the sort of architectural shambles which I became quite used to as the season went on. Lawrence Hourahane, the assistant secretary, who seemed to be doing a good job of being everywhere at once, gave me the guided tour leading me through the rabbit warren of little rooms up on to the roof, across some duckboards to a small turret which was the BBC commentary position and where he left a scribbled note for Andrew Hignell, the statistician who knows all that is to be known about Glamorgan cricket. The note said, 'Bronwen was here.' The view is magnificent.

From there we went down to the press and scorer's box where the Glamorgan scorer, Byron Denning, gave me a humbug, determinedly not giving one to Mr Hourahane, who was obviously being held responsible for the behaviour of the *Telegraph* correspondent's dog. This may be a libel, but I was given to understand that it was the *Telegraph* man's dog. It had been sick on the carpet, though 'carpet' is being a bit generous. It might have been a carpet once, but not for some years. It now lay bundled in a corner, and Mr Denning, who is also secretary of the Ebbw Vale Cricket Club, wanted it removed. 'I'm very fond of dogs,' he said irritably, 'but I think it's ridiculous to bring one to the press box to watch cricket.' The censure sounded all the better for being delivered in a heavy Welsh accent.

Retreating, we took a cup of tea in the players' dining-room, where I was pleased to see the nut-brown wrinkly figure of P. B. Wight who had come to umpire. I used to watch him play for Somerset. Although the pavilion was being used as a cricket pavilion, it reeked of rugby. Practically all the photos and all the mementoes concern Swansea RFC. Almost the only cricketing things were a photo of Gilbert Parkhouse being presented to King George VI at Lord's and a cartoon of Tony Lewis and Majid Khan, the only time two Glamorgan players have captained opposing teams – England and Pakistan – in a Test match. I can't think many counties could boast as much.

Outside, Mr Hourahane passed among the crowd saying, 'The public address system is not working, but Glamorgan have won the toss and elected to bat.' Luckily the crowd was on the small side, though not as small as the crowd for the Zimbabwe match. Then they took nineteen pounds on the gate the first day, so Mr Hourahane decided to let people in free for the next two. The result was that even fewer turned up. They're not stupid, the Welsh – they know that it's wise to look a gift horse in the mouth. At this point Byron Denning turned up to say that they'd got the name of the Leicester scorer wrong and – he asked this very pointedly – had Mr Hourahane made the hotel booking for next week and checked to ensure the place existed? Mr Hourahane went rather red at this and admitted that in Edinburgh, where they were playing Scotland, they had arrived late at night to find their rooms given away, and in Hove they had found the shutters up because the respectable three-star hotel had gone bust since they made the booking.

From the office to the left of the pavilion we could look right across the Bristol channel to North Somerset and the Quantocks. The other day, apparently, HMS *Glamorgan* was in port, and when the officers came to the ground it was so clear that you could see what crops were being grown in each different field.

Another faintly tall Swansea story, attributed like so many items of South Wales folklore to Wilfred Wooller, is the notion that when the tide comes in the pitch changes colour. I put this to the St Helen's groundsman, Richard Stevens, but he said that although the ground was unusual that was not an effect he had noticed. The main problem is that it is so sandy. Later on, in the lunch interval, to my horror, he took out a pen-knife to demonstrate this, but despite hacking a sizeable chunk out of his turf we did not strike sand. 'Obviously doing my job better than I thought,' he said.

Mr Stevens is a tall sunburned figure with a golden beard, and you might have guessed that he had been a groundsman all his adult life except for a spell in the Guards. He started at Blundells School in his native Tiverton, broke off for a spell with the Coldstream Guards, came back, moved to Monmouth School, was poached by Glamorgan to look after Sophia Gardens, the county ground in Cardiff, went to

Worcester where he won the Groundsman of the Year Award, and then came to Swansea to succeed George Clement.

The great problem with the ground is the joint use. Part of the cricket square actually extends from the dead ball line to the goal posts. One of his headaches is the maddening little holes left by the players' studs. The ones left from their lining up behind the posts when a goal is being kicked are bad enough, but he has a fit each time there is a push-over try. He also has some difficulty with rugby supporters who sit in the stand for the match and then walk over to the club house for a pint after the game. The cricket square is on the direct route and he has to try to educate members to go round it. Fences and ropes are not an answer because they apparently challenge people to hurdle them. When they do they invariably fall heavily and make a mess of his wicket.

For an hour or so I sat happily listening to groundsman's lore. The sixty tons of sand that go on to the rugby pitch at season's end; the two and a half hundredweight of Surrey loam with which he top-dresses his wickets; the daily mowing of the outfield; cutting the wickets to three-sixteenths of an inch; pleasing Glamorgan *and* Swansea,

The Cricketers.

who play their South Wales League matches at St Helen's too – not to mention the Lord's Taverners and the annual firework display on November 5th; the sterility of 'marl'; the rigorous demands of the authorities at Lord's; the mixed blessing of working for the council (it's a council ground and the clubs only rent).

Then we walked across behind the hospitality tents, pausing to exclaim over two patches of dead brown grass where the tea ladies had emptied scalding water. They would have to be replaced with fresh turf. There was fresh grass at the entrance to the rugger players' tunnel, worn down by the regular entrances and exits. 'Floreat Swansea' said the legend below the coat of arms.

By Fred's Shed, the public bar where Fred was once the licensee, we found George Clement, Richard Stevens's predecessor, sitting on an empty beer crate. I asked him about the Wooller tale of the changing colour when the tide came in. He laughed at this and said that it wasn't so, but that when the tide came in it brought salty breezes which made the ball move in the air and off the seam. He'd noticed that his glasses always misted up when the tide came in, and he described graphically where each one of Sobers's sixes landed, and recalled the 31,000 who came for a famous West Indies match and how, in the old days, the touring teams had to hunt out a drink on those dry Welsh Sundays. Somehow they had always succeeded.

This was a cue for a pint ourselves, so we went to the Cricketers and drank Ansell's. A good cricketing pub with more cricketing mementoes and pictures of Wilf and the rest than you see in the pavilion. The place mats are old scoresheets of famous Glamorgan games, a series of ten. All of them were rather wonderful and I enjoyed reading about the victory over Simpson's Australians of '64. Best of all, however, was 'The Amazing Match' of '51 when Glamorgan and South Africa had tied the first innings and then, chasing 148, the tourists were 54 for nought at tea. Then the Welsh took all ten wickets for 29, McConnon did a hat-trick and 25,000 supporters sang 'Land of My Fathers' and took a spontaneous collection for the victors and I wished that I had been there.

But I had a good day nonetheless. Younis hit a splendid straight six into the vice-presidents' yellow plastic seats and Javed made 89 and came into the office in shorts and a T-shirt which said 'Cheeky Jewellers, Sharjah, Dubai' and said that it was scandalous to get out for 89 and he should have made 189. Rodney Ontong weighed in with 56, and they were able to declare at 289 for six.

I took a taxi back to the station. We drove very fast to catch the train, and the driver told me in lilting Swansea accents how he had played professional cricket himself but a wound with the Army in Malaya had put paid to that. At a cross roads we got stuck behind a dithering driver and he blew the horn and shouted out to the passers-by: 'I wouldn't let 'er drive sheep.' Again I thought of Dylan Thomas – and again as he ogled a pretty girl on the pavement. He turned to me a moment later and asked if I'd been to the Gnoll at Neath. 'Finer ground than St Helen's. Older too. W. G. Grace played there. Got a pair, he did.'

I thought he was having me on, but later I checked and it was true. The year was 1868 and the twenty-year-old W.G. was playing at Neath for the United South of England. He made nought in the first innings and nought in the second.

So maybe he was right and I should have gone to the Gnoll. But I'd still settle for St Helen's even though the dog was sick on the carpet and there was no vacancy at Mrs Evans's and the grass stays just as green even when the tide comes in.

EDGBASTON

'A *not wholly resolved
compromise between
town and country*'

I had never realised, until I went to Edgbaston, that P. G. Wodehouse used to wear a Warwickshire tie. Dulwich, Le Touquet and Long Island are the localities I associate with Wodehouse, but there in the club room of the Edgbaston pavilion is a letter from the old boy to Leslie Deakins, who was then the secretary of Warwickshire. 'How awfully good of you to send me the Warwickshire tie,' wrote Wodehouse. 'It was just in time, for today I have to go out to lunch (a thing I do about once a year these days), and now I shall be able to dazzle all beholders. On these occasions I never wear any tie except for the Warwickshire, and the old one was beginning to show its years.' This was in 1974, when he was well into his nineties.

The plot thickens if you wander across the room, glancing out at the cricket through the enormous plate glass windows, and look at another glass case in which you will find what might properly be described as Jeeves's ball. This is not an unsavoury relic of Bertie Wooster's batman, but the cricket ball with which the Warwickshire bowler Percy Jeeves took seven Worcester wickets for 34 runs. That was in 1913, the year Jeeves took 106 wickets for the county. You can see him in the back row of the 1913 team photograph, a small, rather dapper man with all three blazer buttons done up very tight. His contemporaries thought he might become one of the great bowlers, but he was killed in the Great War – only to live on in the fiction of P. G. Wodehouse.

Wodehouse evidently saw him play against Gloucester at the Cheltenham Festival and took a fancy to the name. Hence a great comic character. And hence Wodehouse and the blue and gold and silver necktie.

For the record, Wodehouse played cricket for the Dulwich College eleven. The school magazine recorded: 'Bowled well against Tonbridge but did nothing else. Does not use his head at all. A poor bat and very slack field.' Later he did well with his leg breaks while in a German internment camp during the war. The real-life Jeeves scored 1,193 runs at an average of 16.12 in his tragically short career and took 194 wickets at 20.20 apiece. He bowled fast medium and hit hard. He once put a six clean over the pavilion.

It was quiet when I visited the Birmingham ground, which was scarcely surprising because the county's opponents were Zimbabwe. As Alan Smith, the Warwickshire secretary, remarked, Zimbabwe could bat a bit but their bowling was 'rather less good than most counties'. The first day had been ruined by rain and Warwickshire were cruising to over three hundred for the loss of only two wickets. The members in the club room seemed a little perplexed.

'Where exactly *is* Zimbabwe?' asked one.

'It used to be Northern Rhodesia,' replied another, getting it not quite right but speaking with an enviable air of authority.

'I would have expected to see some coloured people,' said the first member, peering out at the light tan faces of the Zimbabwe men.

His companion continued to speak authoritatively, though I wasn't sure whether he was still muddling the opposition with Zambia or not. 'Football's the national game over there,' he said, 'but they're sending some coaches into the coloured areas to get them to change to cricket. They're hoping for Test status before long.'

If that happens they will certainly have the flag for it. Mr Mugabe's government have come up with a very exotic affair with a large star on the left and alternating green, red, orange and black stripes. It looks a bit like a remnant of one of Ian Botham's new blazers. At Edgbaston it was flying over the old stand at the Rugby Football Ground end.

This is one of the few old and unconverted bits of a very prosperous, modern-feeling ground. Until 1929 Edgbaston was one of the Test match venues, usually alternating with Trent Bridge. But in the thirties Trent Bridge benefited from the generosity of Sir Julien Cahn, while Edgbaston stagnated. No Tests were played there in the thirties and the team was stolidly unsuccessful. Support was always difficult to find, partly for geographical reasons. Hit a six over the River Rea and it will land in Worcestershire; and much of Birmingham is in Staffordshire. The original centre of Warwickshire cricket was in the county's heartland at Leamington, where the professionals Parr and Wisden had a ground. Edgbaston would have an easier time if they played a Brummie XI instead of a Warwickshire one.

'They don't know which county they belong to in Birmingham,' says Leslie Deakins. 'It was difficult developing an allegiance.'

Mr Deakins joined the club in 1928, became secretary in 1944 and only retired in 1976. Loyal and long service is a characteristic of cricket but even so the performance of the Warwickshire secretaries has been rather astonishing. R. V. Ryder was secretary from 1899 until 1944, when Mr Deakins took over, and he was succeeded in 1976 by Alan Smith, who captained the team that won the 1971 county championship. Mr Smith is still in his forties, so there is every chance of him still being at the crease in the centenary of Ryder's original appointment. Even as it stands, only three secretaries in eighty-six years is quite an achievement.

Mr Deakins was on good form during the Zimbabwe match, and produced memories of the ground going back to 1921, when he first came in a school party to watch Warwick Armstrong's Australians. 'The master would only take six boys,' he says, 'and three of you sat one side of him and three the other. When you went to the toilet you went in order, and never more than one at a time. That was when I learned the first golden rule: no one goes on the playing area. You

only go there as of right – when you're playing. That's been forgotten now like so many things. All these people nowadays wearing ties and blazer badges they're not entitled to ... but there's nothing you can do about it.'

Seven years later he was back at Edgbaston as a member of staff. An advertisement appeared in the local paper for 'an assistant to the secretary of a sports club'. He had no idea what club it was, but was pleased when he found out. It was, in many ways, a peculiar job – particularly when viewed from the mid-eighties.

'One of my first jobs was to ask F. S. Gough-Calthorpe if he wanted the visiting amateurs in with him.' Gough-Calthorpe, the Warwick-shire captain, whose family owned half Birmingham, including the Edgbaston ground, could either invite the opposing amateurs to share his dressing-room or ask them to use the one set aside for visitors. 'He'd always say, "Who are we playing?", and I'd tell him and he'd say "Oh yes" or "Oh no!" depending on whether he approved or not.' Some amateurs were chosen for the team simply so that they could be acceptable company for the captain on Sundays. During an away match before the advent of Sunday cricket, this could be an important consideration! When Mr Deakins came into the game most teams had two or three amateurs, mostly 'for companionship'. Yorkshire often had only the one as captain; Middlesex had four or five; wayward, impecunious Somerset as many, he thinks, as seven or eight.

His next captain was R. E. S. Wyatt, cousin of Woodrow. 'Bob never changed,' he says. 'He was a cricketer first, last and all the time.' Of other early players he remembers the incomparable William Quaife, who came back in '28 for a last encore and scored a hundred against Derby; and Len Bates, ever dapper, whose cap and blazer are now in the pavilion, as an example of what the well-dressed cricketer wore. Tiger Smith kept wicket. And there was Norman Partridge and George Paine.

Another memorable figure was his first boss, R. V. Ryder. Mr Ryder didn't think the Edgbaston ground a safe place in which to spend winter. For a start there was no electricity. Electricity didn't arrive until after the war. For this and other reasons Mr Ryder wintered in the city. So every September a strange little procession could be seen proceeding from Edgbaston to Number One, Albert Street, Birmingham. In front was Bill Mullett's horse. Bill Mullett was a corn and seed merchant who grazed his horse in a paddock next to the ground. Mullett led the horse. Behind it came a covered cart with all the papers from the Edgbaston office. On the cart rode young Deakins. And ten yards behind, on foot, followed R. V. Ryder, secretary of Warwickshire CCC, ready to pick up anything that fell from the cart. And every April, the little procession returned – an annual harbinger of summer.

During the war Mr Deakins served with the Navy, mainly at Scapa Flow. When he returned, and was promoted to succeed R. V. Ryder, he found that he had an unusually go-ahead and also rich new president: Doctor Thwaite, now immortalised by 'The Thwaite Gates' and 'The Thwaite Scoreboard'. 'I want,' Thwaite told him, 'to be president, but president of what? I want to be president of something worth being president of.' Thwaite had two specific ambitions. He wanted a side that could emulate the 1911 Warwickshire team and win the championship. And he wanted a ground which would once again stage Test matches. It is a matter of record that in 1951 Warwickshire were county champions and that in 1957 they started to stage Test matches again.

The team building was helped by having Tom Dollery as captain. Dollery had been at Edgbaston since 1934 and was one of the most astute leaders of his time. Otherwise the nucleus was small. Mr Deakins says that he personally scoured the most obvious nursery – the Minor Counties – and recruited men like Dick Spooner and Alan Townsend from as far afield as Durham, Berkshire and Cornwall. The improvements to the ground were made possible by a phenomenally successful football pool scheme. The idea had been pioneered by the Roman Catholic Church, and in the cricket world by Worcester. The Warwickshire authorities went to Worcester, learned how the scheme

worked and adapted it with such success that they built up to 10,000
agents and cleared £180,000 a year.

Mr Deakins played a prominent part in all this and he remains a
regular visitor to the ground as well as running the old county cricketers' association which exists 'to bring together both in season and
out of season in good fellowship and in the true spirit and tradition of
cricket those who have played first-class county cricket for Warwickshire.' The Deakins view is not always orthodox, but is almost always
robust.

He regrets, for instance, the passing of the amateur and says that
the legislation which abolished the distinction between 'gentlemen' and
'players' in 1962 represented the single most significant change in the
game in his lifetime. But he defends one-day cricket. He thinks the
successful players in the one-day game play just as 'correctly' as their
predecessors; and for many people the three-day game was a disaster.
'I can recall people coming to me and saying "You won the toss and
batted, and all I saw on Saturday was Jack Hobbs or Frank Woolley
fielding...." They didn't like that.' They liked it even less when they
had to go to work on Monday and Hobbs or Woolley played a classic
innings.

Mr Deakins is also good on committees. 'A body of the unfit elected
by the unwilling to do the unnecessary,' he says – while making it
clear he is not talking about his own county's committee. Then, in the
next breath, he asked if I knew the classic definition of a committee,
which I didn't. 'A committee is like a bunch of bananas,' he explained,
'– they start green, turn yellow and in the end there isn't a straight
one in the bunch.'

Critics of change have complained that Edgbaston has become 'a
concrete mausoleum'. Mr Deakins nods in part agreement and says
that would be inappropriate at Worcester or Taunton, but here in
Birmingham....

The huge executive suite to the left of the pavilion as you look
towards the city is the most obvious example of the 'concrete mausoleum' approach. It is a long way from thatched roof and roses over
the door of the pub, but it works. One hundred companies pay an
£800 annual membership which entitles them to eight admissions on
any day. Even during the Zimbabwe game sixty lunches had been
booked. When I wandered in, businessmen and their clients waited in
salivating queues for cuts off various joints. 'We have two ballrooms
here,' said Alan Smith laconically, and I wasn't entirely sure whether
he approved or not. Ordinary members of the Warwickshire club use
the bar and restaurant below. It has just as good a view but is not
quite so luxurious. Stewards do occasionally have trouble with non-
Executive Club members climbing in over the railings from below and
ordering drinks on other people's accounts. Not cricket.

The stands are large and glassy, and not particularly beautiful, but there is a lot of leafiness about, and the astute club owns twenty-odd acres all round, so no high-rise blocks shut out the light and you can see the towers of Brum away in the distance. I feel about this place that it is a not wholly resolved compromise between town and country, trade and aristocracy, progress and conservatism. On the walls of the club room the photographs of the 7th Earl of Warwick (by Vivienne of London) and Brigadier Sir Richard Anstruther-Gough-Calthorpe share space with Dr Thwaite and Mr Ludford C. Docker. Edgbaston displays a charmingly idealist poem from Haverford, near Philadelphia, full of cricketing references like 'the last over which we all must face' and 'the captain who has gone before'.

> Could you imagine this whole earth could yield
> A spot more beautiful than our old cricket field?

I prefer the pithier reality of the original rules of the old Birmingham Club, especially the one which says: 'A member beginning a game and not remaining to the end shall forfeit sixpence.'

P. G. Wodehouse could have built a lovely short story from that, with Percy Jeeves bowling from in front of the pavilion and Bertie Wooster forfeiting a sixpence for not remaining to the end. I wonder what happened to the old boy's Warwickshire tie? It's not in the glass case.

HARROW

*'Allotted as "a place
of exercise"
by George III'*

There are two Harrows. One is the John Betjeman Harrow, far out on the Metropolitan line, a land of semi-detached houses built by a giant with a set of Minibrix, the Lego of the forties and fifties. Here and there is an Italian restaurant with music on Friday and Saturday nights and all roads lead to Wembley stadium. The vivid yellow signs of the AA are stuck to every lamp-post.

In the middle of this Metroland there is an island. It would be too fanciful to call it Camelot, but it has something of St Michael's Mount about it as you look out from the window of the northbound train just before Harrow and Wealdstone station. It is steep-sided with narrow streets, a mish-mash of private houses of all periods, some impressive, rather monumental public buildings and a tall church steeple to crown it. This English hill-village is the other Harrow: the Harrow which educated Byron and Palmerston and Baldwin and Churchill; the Harrow of 'Eton and Harrow', as evocative and inescapable a combination as Fortnum and Mason or Bubble and Squeak.

Even the graffiti at the bottom of the hill seemed Harrovian. 'Happy birthday debs' said the one on the left (referring, I hoped, to debutantes rather than Deborah), while the one on the right said 'Ahoy Anybody?'

In fact I approached the wrong way. The green emptiness at the foot of that side of the hill is for rugger. The cricket is played at the foot of the other side. Always has been, Harrovians tell you, though the school was founded in 1571 and serious cricket did not start until over two hundred years later.

The Eleven was playing Haileybury and having much the better of it. The Haileybury coach said 'Reg's Carefree Holiday Tours' on the back, which did not strike me as altogether propitious. Harrow had put them in on a dampish day and skittled them out for 83. Harrow's opening batsmen looked comfortable. It had been a good toss to win, but in any case Harrow were a strong side. They had already beaten the old boys by ten wickets and MCC by five. As for schools, they had squeaked home by one wicket against Radley, but comfortably disposed of St Edwards, Oxford (98 runs), Winchester (seven wickets), Malvern (five wickets) and Charterhouse (an innings and 108 runs). Only Eton were left.

Like a county ground, Harrow's 'Sixth Form Ground' has impressive gates, dedicated in this case to 'M.C. Kemp, 1861-1951, Master in charge of cricket for thirty-three years.' The inscription goes on to say that the 'wide extension' of the playing fields was due to his 'energy and foresight'. But there is an even more impressive plaque a little further up the drive. It is on the wall of the Old Harrovian Field House Club and it says: 'Whereas by an Act passed in the reign of His

Majesty George III this piece of ground was allotted to the Governors of Harrow School for a Place of Exercise for the Scholars and provision ordered that no road or Highway should be made, maintained or supported in, over or through the same.'

It is quirkily predictable that Harrow should have a cricket ground protected by a Georgian Act of Parliament. In the same way I was not wholly surprised to learn that their first two cricket professionals were Wilfred Rhodes and Patsy Hendren. The present holder of that title is Percy Davis, a twinkling septuagenarian, resplendent in his Northants sweater and Northants blazer and Oxford and Bucks Light Infantry tie. I found him by the nets, talking to the master in charge of cricket, Bill Snowden, who played in Majid Khan's Cambridge University team. These two and Peter Ward, the groundsman, who started work at the school forty-seven years ago, make up the key triumvirate in modern Harrow cricket. Peter Ward succeeded his father, who also had forty-seven years in the job.

It was he who took me over to the Harrow Field House Club. The crowd was sparse - a local or two stood on the pavement and leaned

65

reflectively on the fence; a few boys and masters; a very occasional parent, and one family group finishing a picnic at a table laid with a white cloth. They had bottles of red and white wine, and although I didn't wish to pry it didn't look as if it came from Tesco. Nor did I eavesdrop, but I couldn't help catching '... and found he had to educate six children out of earned income. And that isn't easy.' Strange how a throw-away reminder of the cost of certain things brings out the socialist in one.

The club is part dressing-room for visiting teams, part viewing platform and drinking den (good bar) for Old Harrovians, and part museum. The old photographs, the bats, the scorecards, the relics are as impressive as most counties'. The single most extraordinary revelation for me was that A.C. MacLaren of Lancashire and England and F.S. Jackson of Yorkshire and England both played in the same Harrow School eleven just under a hundred years ago. A similar contemporary coincidence is unthinkable. The Harrow triumvirate could only think of two current first-class cricketers from Eton and Harrow:

Barclay and Pigott. A.N. Hornby ('O my Hornby and my Barlow') was a Harrovian; and so were Robin Marlar and Aidan Crawley, once a Labour and then a Conservative MP who made 156 out of 257 for Kent against Essex – an innings described by Lord Harris, who was watching, as 'the most remarkable ever played'. Charabanc loads of Crawleys have been to Harrow, all of them apparently cricketers. A Crawley XI played Lords and Commons on 1 June 1965. Viscount Monckton was in the 1910 Lords team along with the future Field Marshal Alexander of Tunis. How debonair he looks in his photograph. The Earl of Bessborough and The Hon. R. Grimston played in '84 and founded I Zingari later. There is a Spy cartoon of Bessborough hanging in the Field House Club, and nearby they have Bessborough's umbrella, very ramshackle and ill-furled, just as it is in the picture. My housemaster, whose father was headmaster and who married *his* housemaster's daughter, played during the war. P.C. Boissier. 1941.

Best of all is a huge oil painting entitled 'The Interval, 1905'. It was discovered in a garage in Orpington, and shows the crowd outside the Lord's pavilion in presumably the lunch or tea break during the Eton and Harrow match. Hundreds of toffs in toppers with frilled ladies. You catch a real sense of a past world from it – even though as a painting it is not particularly good. That was a time, you feel, when the nation's business – whether in Parliament or the City or the law courts – adjourned for the day, and the great and the good went off to watch their old schools play cricket. I did not check to see if Stanley Baldwin, then the adopted Tory candidate for Kidderminster, was present. Baldwin's biographer says that of his contemporaries at the school four became viceroys, ten bishops, twelve colonial governors, a dozen ambassadors, seventeen judges, thirty-three privy councillors and sixty-four generals. Looking at that painting of the 1905 game, you can well believe it.

If Harrow's place in the world has slipped in recent years, the cricket at least is holding up. Peter Ward likes to prepare true wickets. 'You can't have the ball flying about. I want them to be able to play off the front foot.' And Percy Davis instils the basics to such effect that since he arrived the record in that all-important Eton match is three-two in his favour. And there have been moral victories too. He says he cried after one game. Harrow declared with only two wickets down and bowled Eton out. Harrow went in again and once more declared after losing only two wickets. Eton got the runs with two wickets left. Percy still can't believe it. 'They lost eighteen wickets. We lost four. And they won.'

On another occasion, when the Lord's wicket was being dug up in order to get rid of the infamous ridge, Eton played on the Harrow Sixth Form Ground and managed to get them all out by bowling, Percy Davis alleges, about forty overs an hour. John Barclay, the Eton captain, now of Sussex, almost completely dispensed with his run-up.

Percy was heartbroken. But the '85 side was a good one, with a terrific pair of fast bowlers called Pethers and Fox. Even Percy Davis, who made his first fifty against Larwood and Voce in 1933, spoke highly of Pethers and Fox.

We had tea in the professionals' room at the back of the pavilion. Bill Snowden, Percy Davis, the umpires, a couple of stiff-upper-lipped Haileybury beaks (Harrow got the runs with only two wickets down) and a lady artist who specialises in painting cricket grounds. There were old caps, striped and quartered and hooped, hanging on pegs along with Percy's own maroon Northants one, and we had sandwiches and cup cakes and milky tea from a huge tin pot. Each year, agreed Bill and Percy and the Haileybury beaks, they see boys who should go on to first-class cricket. Percy Davis said he had had one the other year, Matthew Fosh, who should have captained England, but he gave up cricket after a few games for Essex and rode a horse round Canada. Or something like that.

Nowadays Harrovians have to earn a living – especially if they're educating their young out of earned income. And you can't pay Harrow fees from an average county player's salary. But that doesn't mean the Harrow standard has dropped. Next week I Zingari. Then Eton and Lord's. 'It's my seventieth year,' said Percy, 'and the 150th of the match. If we can pull that off I'll be happy. It's what I live for.'

Horris Hill

*'You have to make
it clear that
it is a hard ball
and a lethal bat'*

Prep school cricket is like village cricket – in terms of skill it comes very low in the scale of things. In every other respect it is the best possible cricket. The setting is nearly always rural and wooded, with a small pavilion probably presented by a rich parent; the wicket will have been prepared properly by the school groundsman, supervised by the headmaster, who will almost certainly be a decent club cricketer who just missed a Blue; the game will be short and to the point and highly competitive; and the team teas will include sticky buns.

I would have written about my old school's ground in the lea of the Quantocks five miles west of Taunton. Before the school was evacuated there from Weymouth during the war it had belonged to the Boles family. Boles baronets held cricket weekends in the twenties and thirties. Robertson-Glasgow played. The pavilion was thatched.

Anyhow I can't write about that prep school ground because it is now the home of the Bishop's Lydeard village team. Instead I paid a visit to Horris Hill.

Horris Hill is a Victorian foundation a few miles south of Newbury, and just off the Winchester road. Partly because of Horris Hill's geographical proximity to Winchester, the school's stock in trade is preparing boys for the Winchester College entrance and scholarship exams. Malcolm Innes, the headmaster, gave me a list of the Horris Hill exam results for the seven years between September 1978 and July 1985. It is a fairly stunning document. 'Winchester Entrance: 48 boys took the examination and they all passed.' Seven boys won Winchester scholarships; three got exhibitions. Fifty-four of their boys passed into Eton, and of 138 who took the common entrance only three failed to get into the school of their choice. A note at the bottom of this catalogue says rather austerely, 'Horris Hill has no entrance examination at present. Sometimes, however, boys come to Horris Hill who might be better suited at a school where remedial help is part of the normal curriculum. In such cases parents are advised of the situation but in no case does Horris Hill insist on a boy's removal to another school.'

For many years Horris Hill was a family business, run by the Stows. Mr Innes filled me in on the school's academic background but preferred to leave it to the two surviving Stows, Jimmy and Sandy, to tell me about cricket and about history. They still live near the school which they used to run and when they came into the present headmaster's drawing-room I found myself irresistibly reminded of my own prep school days. Tweedy and beaming, amusing and amused, they seemed the epitome of the prep school master. A breed quite unlike 'public school master' or 'state school master', being quirkier, more relaxed, less harassed. I think it is because when their little charges leave at the age of thirteen all their futures seem so rosy. It is only later that the doubts start to seep in. I wonder whether there isn't more optimism in a prep school than anywhere else in life. Or, if you're being hostile, more smugness. Two sides, I suppose, of the same coin.

'Our dear father,' they said, 'was a cricketer, and Horris Hill did cricket and classics and very little else. There were no frills at all.'

The most famous Horris Hill cricketer was D.R. Jardine himself, and Jardine captained the school in one of the most famous or infamous matches in prep school cricket history. It was one of the few occasions on which both schools were led by future captains of England. The opposition was Summer Fields, of Oxford, captained by G.O.B. Allen. Summer Fields was an Eton prep, and rivalry between the two places was – and still remains – intense. That year – 1914 – Summer Fields were unbeaten but it was generally acknowledged that Horris Hill were much the stronger side.

The Summer Fields cricket master, Mr Alington, therefore decided that his side would bat first and stonewall. The usual convention in prep school cricket was that the side batting first should, if not all out, then declare sportingly enough to allow the opposition at least a notional chance of getting the runs. Mr Alington was enough of a realist to know that if he did that Horris Hill would get the runs.

Summer Fields won the toss and batted, but despite Mr Alington's orders the wickets fell steadily until at number eight, Christopher Hollis, later a well-known Member of Parliament, author, wit and poet, strode to the wicket. 'As a general rule,' said Hollis, 'I was the most impatient of batsmen. I hit out wildly, usually succumbing to a very early ball and, if my luck happened to be in, making a few but making them very quickly.'

Under orders from his skipper, G.O.B. Allen, and Mr Alington, Hollis put his head down and blocked away for two hours and eighteen runs – an obdurate performance of almost unprecedented tedium for prep school cricket. His only aberration was a leg-side four off Jardine himself. When they were finally dismissed there were only twenty minutes of play left and the result was a draw.

At the end of the game Jardine was, in the words of one Stow brother, 'in floods of tears'. The other Stow looked sage. 'And that really meant something in those days,' he said. 'Nowadays you're in tears if you've lost your pencil.'

Fifty years later, after two world wars and the bodyline tour which he dominated, Jardine bumped into Hollis and the two men shared a drink. Both remembered the epic Horris Hill – Summer Fields encounter of 1914, and Jardine was prepared to forgive Hollis on the grounds that he was acting under orders. But he never forgave Mr Alington.

More than seventy years after the event the Summer Fields game is still the most important feature of the Horris Hill calendar. But 1914 has not been quite forgotten.

There are 160 boys in the school, and on the afternoon I called each single one was playing cricket. They play cricket six afternoons a week, for as Jimmy and Sandy Stow pointed out, there is no more effective way of getting that number out in the fresh air and out of mischief.

The two Stows and I wandered across the croquet lawn and past the dovecote towards 'The Top Field', the First Eleven ground which had been cleared from bracken and gorse in the 1890s. On the junior ground scores of little boys in grey flannel bags batted and bowled.

'Peterson and Wood!' shouted Sandy Stow at two boys, 'Move away from the batsman or you'll be hurt.' He turned to me apologetically. 'You have to make it clear to them,' he said, smiling, 'that it's a hard ball and a lethal bat.'

At the corner of the Top Field little boys turned and wheeled, youngish masters demonstrated leg breaks and forward defensive shots, and one boy was summoned to talk to us because his name was Powell and his grandfather had been headmaster when I was at Sherborne. He was very polite, stood at attention with his hands at his side and said 'sir' repeatedly.

It was a pretty ground, surrounded by trees and with a small wooden pavilion presented by a parent. The following weekend Jim Swanton's 'Arabs' were due – a highlight of the season when the pitch is ringed with cars and picnics. The Stows told some funny stories about Swanton, especially about him captaining R. W. V. Robins. When someone hit a dolly at Swanton, Robins shouted, 'Ten to one on the ball', and Jim dropped the catch and stomped off in dudgeon, leaving instructions that Robins was not to be put on to bowl under any circumstances. According to the Stows it was weeks before they spoke again.

The wicket had been beautifully prepared – close cut and rolled again and again. There wasn't a mark on it. Nor a daisy nor a weed of any kind.

Ian Peebles was an old boy. And H. A. Pawson. And A. G. McDonnell, who wrote *England their England*. Hubert Doggart was a father. So was 'Charlie' Fry, C.B.'s grandson, and R. E. S. Wyatt, who was remembered for taking the father's match so terribly seriously. He scored more than fifty and obviously did not want to be out.

They take their cricket seriously at Horris Hill, but it can be taken too seriously. They don't like chaps to be big-headed. The Stows remembered a boy called Lee who got the second scholarship at Winchester and was captain of the eleven. Just after he'd won the scholarship the school played West Downs – old rivals like Summer Fields. Lee made a hundred and took six wickets, including a hat-trick. In the bus on the way home he was inclined to be a little bumptious and noisy. The master in charge responded in the prescribed Horris Hill fashion: 'Shut up Lee!', he said, 'I don't know what on earth you've got to be so pleased about.'

Cricket is compulsory at prep schools, and prep school cricket is as good as ever it was. By contrast I spent several bleak summer mornings watching my son play cricket with the London Oratory Under-13 side.

At first glance their grounds are at least as impressive as those of Horris Hill. The flat acres of Barn Elms running along the Thames opposite the Fulham football ground are lush, regularly mown and attractively treed.

The Oratory is not the only school entitled to play here. The grounds are owned and run by the Inner London Education Authority, which means that any one of the ILEA schools in the south-west of London can use it. In practice, however, it is the Oratory home patch.

The Under-13s were not as cultured and coached as the Horris Hill boys. Unless they play for a local club they tend to play no more than once or twice a week, because the cramped school grounds behind the Chelsea football ground only have room for two nets and Barn Elms are a bus ride away. But the captain, Greg Neame, was a useful all-rounder who played for the London schools in his age group; Hamish Gunasekera, whose father was almost the only other regular parental supporter, bowled quite fast and batted stylishly; and the others weighed in successfully enough. Some games, notably the one in which the Oratory dismissed Gunnersbury for 19, were over almost before they began.

The greatest contrast between Horris Hill and the Oratory is in the wicket. Writing in the *Oratorian*, Mr Matthews, the Oratory cricket master, commented on a Barn Elms wicket that 'looked as if, and played as if, it had been prepared three days before.' He told me that the Barn Elms wickets were so bumpy that it wasn't safe to play a First Eleven game on them.

I thought of all the care, all the rolling and mowing and dressing that went into the wickets at Horris Hill and Harrow, of the importance their coaches attached to getting boys to learn how to play safely off the front foot. And I reflected also that tomorrow's professional cricketers will not be coming from schools like Horris Hill and Harrow but from state comprehensives like the Oratory. Perhaps the ILEA doesn't approve of cricket. I dare say they think it's sexist and elitist. At all events it is a pity. Barn Elms is a great fifty acres of flat grass on a prime site. With a sightscreen or two and a heavy roller; a proper slip-catching machine; perhaps some parental enthusiasm ... with all these the Barn Elms grounds could be as good as anything at Harrow or Horris Hill. As it is they're second-rate – proof that in a socially divided society you can't have real equality of opportunity even at cricket.

BRISTOL

*'Billowing canvas,
clients in business suits,
and a man in a
Matabeleland blazer'*

I was more than usually apprehensive about Bristol cricket ground because of the David Foot – Alan Gibson school of cricket writing. Mr Foot and Mr Gibson sometimes appear to have lived all their lives on West Country cricket grounds and they both write interestingly about more than the cricket. David Collier, Gloucester's secretary, had suggested I visit Bristol during the Australians' match in July so that I could savour 'the character and atmosphere of the ground during a festival'. Other county secretaries tended to suggest I see them when there was only a man and a dog on the ground, so this was refreshing advice. On the other hand somewhere between Sunningdale and Bracknell I got to David Foot's report in the *Guardian* and read, 'The Bristol ground was full of billowing canvas, appearing far more intimate and carnival-like than usual.'

I was immediately dispirited. I was going to get a false impression, conned into thinking that at Bristol the canvas always billows and it is forever carnival time. Foot and Gibson would know better than that. Perhaps, however, the Lord Mayor of Bristol would be there as it was a special occasion. I had travelled to Venice with the Lord Mayor a few months before on the Orient Express, no less. And I had been much impressed with the gold chain of office which he wore for dinner parked outside Paris. Some flunkey or other had told me that not only were there more Georgian houses in Bristol than in Bath (I am still sceptical about this) but that Bristol still had a coach and horses – Lord Mayor, for the use of. Perhaps there would be a Lord Mayor's procession to the cricket week and I would see him sitting on a throne in front of the billowing canvas acknowledging the plaudits of the crowd.

Alas no. The billowing canvas belonged to Barclays Bank and Harrison Cowley Advertising and British Telecom and Laing. And there was no sign of the Lord Mayor. Nothing but 'clients' in 'business suits'.

It was a special occasion because Gloucester were leading the championship table and their young fast bowler David 'Syd' Lawrence was the leading English wicket-taker. The England side was badly in need of a genuine fast bowler and there was a growing buzz of popular opinion which said that Lawrence should be picked for the Old Trafford Test. The selectors were said to be coming westwards.

I had a lady taxi driver from Temple Meads and I knew I was in the West Country because when she dropped me at the gates she said, 'That'll be two pounds, sixty, my love.' They don't call you 'my love' anywhere but in the west.

The Gloucester gates are inevitable and there is a plaque to celebrate

the greatest of them all – or at least the most famous. 'To commemorate Dr. W.G. Grace, the great cricketer. Born 1848. Died 1915.
This tablet was erected outside his county ground at the centenary of
his birth. 18th July. 1948.' They don't put his vital statistics underneath
but they are in the county yearbook. For the best part of thirty years
at the end of the nineteenth century he captained the county. He scored
22,921 runs for Gloucestershire at an average of 40.64. His highest
score was 318 not out against Yorkshire at Cheltenham in 1876; the
same ground where, a year later, he took seventeen Nottinghamshire
wickets for 89. He hit 51 hundreds and 108 fifties and took 1,349
wickets for an average of 18.43 each. He caught 374 catches and made
four stumpings. So he was more than just a pretty face.

My taxi drive from Temple Meads had left me slightly disoriented
so I set off on what was meant to be a quick perambulation of the
streets around the ground. The centre of Bristol has been Birming-
hammed into office blocks divided from one another by motorways,
but the cricket ground is way up the Gloucester road in Victorian villa
country. Seldom have I seen so many villas: Saltford Villa, Gerard
Villa, Apsley Villa, Cecil Villa. All of them with bow windows and
privet hedges. Here and there a lodge. A lodge is one up from a villa,
bigger and more ornate. Colston Lodge. Sefton Lodge. The roads are
named after cricket opponents. Nottingham Road and Kent Road and
Derby Road. In the grocer's shop there was an advertisement for a
'Very very old lady's bicycle'. Whether it was the bike or the lady who
was so very very old is not important. It caught the spirit of the area
although here and there I spotted CND signs which suggested an influx
of trendier, younger people. The butcher wore a boater but next door
in the greengrocer's a black man in a Rastafarian cap peered suspi-
ciously at the nectarines. Sandringham, Chatsworth, Cabot House.
Who did they think they were fooling, the men of 1890? Did the first
inhabitants cause those grandiose names to be chiselled into the stone
above the door? Or were they foisted on them by the builders? Behind
the net curtains at eleven o'clock in the morning the present inhabitants could be seen sitting in their bow windows with the *Daily Mirror*
open in front of them.

Actually the villas are rather jolly. The most dispiriting part of the
neighbourhood is what used to be Muller's orphanage, great grey
buildings in military monumental. They could easily pass for the old
naval dockyard in somewhere like Malta. The end opposite the pavilion is still designated the Muller's orphanage end, but the buildings
have now been taken over by the Brunel Technical College and Bristol
Polytechnic's Department of Engineering.

By the time I had entered the ground the Australians were batting
and had already lost a wicket. I walked slowly past the hospitality
tents and the hard tennis courts, some of which were in use, past the
press enclosure and the Jessop Tavern at the Orphanage End and

found a seat on the mound. The ground, if not bursting, was quite full.

'Who got the first wicket?' I enquired of my neighbour, a luminous veined pensioner clutching a can of lager. He looked at me as if I were daft.

'No idea,' he said. He was obviously only there for the beer.

'Lawrence,' said a black man in a cap just in front of us. 'Clean bowled.'

Lawrence was bowling from the Orphanage End, a hulking great black man, with a lot of shoulder in his action. A moment or so later he had Wellham well caught by the wicket-keeper. The crowd shouted, a lovely exultant sound, but my neighbour scarcely noticed what had happened.

I had seen the Australian flag before. Curious how they still have that old imperial anachronism with its union flag in the corner. But I had never seen Gloucester's. It is almost as multi-coloured as Zimbabwe's – a blue square bordered by alternating stripes of yellow and chocolate, green and white and red. The county tie is on similar lines. The two fluttered from the pavilion which at least had a wrought iron balcony, a clock tower and a weathervane but was unhappily built in the same style and material as Muller's orphanage.

Outside the pavilion I met Barrie Meyer's brother, up from Bournemouth for the day to see the Australians being umpired by his brother and David Shepherd, and called briefly on David Collier, who seemed extraordinarily harrassed, as well he might. Not just a full house but also a grand dinner at the Dragonara that evening with Gloucester's new patron, the Princess of Wales, as guest of honour.

There is no museum at Bristol. Indeed one staff member told me there could be no question of displaying old bats and balls because people would only steal them. They don't elsewhere. I should have thought Phoenix Assurance, who own the ground, might invest a little cash in a museum. Even in Mr Collier's office the photographs were somewhat faded though I liked the one of W.G. and a young Prince of Wales looking bored and dandified with a boater and cane. Alongside there is a signature of the Doctor's, presumably cut from a letter because it says, simply, 'Yours in haste, W.G. Grace.' In a corner cupboard away from public scrutiny is the ball with which Gilbert Jessop completed his highest score of 286 against Sussex at Brighton and another with which Dennett took the last six Kent wickets for no runs in 1912. Also a gilded version of the scorecard from the Australian match of 1930, which ended in a tie after Goddard and Parker spun Ponsford, Bradman and Co. out for 117 in the final innings.

Outside on the pitch the home side were hustling out the Australian batsmen in fine old style. Graveney had three quick bowlers to play with: Lawrence, a lithe tall West Indian named Courtenay Walsh and a very handy Zimbabwe all-rounder, Kevin Curran. I went to the

members' enclosure to the right of the pavilion and sat behind a middle-aged chap with five children aged around eight or nine. He could have been a father or a prep school master – probably the former as term was over. Father was explaining the picnic lunch like Rat in *The Wind in the Willows*.

'There are five marmite rolls,' he said, 'and five egg rolls. And five peanut butter sandwiches. And some sausages. And four pork pies.'

'I'm going to have a peanut butter,' said one little boy.

'I'm going to have one of everything,' said another.

There was a loud communal shout. Walsh had bowled O'Donnell. Comprehensively. He walked back to the pavilion looking sulky, and the little boys charged off to get his autograph.

A minute or so later the boys were back.

'He told me to fuck off!' exclaimed one, feverishly.

'Peter thought he said "monks off",' said another.

'He was calling everybody "bastards",' said a third.

There was an interesting postscript later when Australia fielded. Jeff Thomson was positioned at third man quite near the small boys. In between balls of Lawson's over he was signing quite happily, one leg against the advertising board for support. He turned round and walked in every time Lawson ran up, then went back to signing. Next over Border moved him to long leg and put O'Donnell at third man. O'Donnell didn't even look at the boys.

During the lunch interval the clients all went under billowing canvas from which many did not emerge until three o'clock, by which time the Australian innings had been wrapped up. As Alan Gibson remarked in the next day's *Times*, 'They must have had quite a shock as, reluctantly, digesting the last mouthful of anchoie suprême and the last sip of Cointreau, they turned round to find Australia all out.'

I must not be unkind to sponsors – lifeblood of the game and all that. Their tents were very pretty, too, though I did hear a couple of older members remonstrating with Mr Collier in the nicest possible way about – essentially – the sponsors getting better treatment than the members. And it was noticeable that a third of the ground was taken up by some eight hundred men (scarcely any women) in the tents, while several thousand were crammed into the remaining two-thirds.

Still, the hoi poloi had a good lunch too. A dozen or so cricket games started up around the boundary and about a hundred of us had a long peer at the wicket to see what it was doing. It looked quite ordinary to me, and when I asked David Bridle, the head groundsman, he said only, 'It's still quite wet out there because it's got so much clay in it. It's obviously doing a bit now and again but it's not so much the wicket as the humidity. You notice that whenever the sun comes out the ball starts hitting the middle of the bat.' I hadn't, but concentrated harder and had to concede he had a point.

The band of the Gloucestershire Regiment, the Glorious Glosters, gave us a reedy selection from *The Sound of Music* and heralded the return of the umpires with a spirited post-horn gallop. I talked to one steward, a young man with a limp moustache who said he wasn't much of a cricketer and that 'skittles is really my game'; and to a programme seller called Doug Knowlson, who used to be a supervisor with Associated British Foods and first watched the county fifty-four years ago. 'Hammond was a treat to watch,' he said. 'He used to walk half-way down the wicket and use his wrists.' He thought Lawrence wasn't ready for England yet. He hadn't even got his county cap. Had anyone ever been capped by England before being capped by their county? I couldn't answer that, and should have asked Henry Blofeld, whom I accosted on the roof by the press box, but instead I asked him about the time he faced the bowling of Keith Miller while a Cambridge undergraduate. He did not seem to have any very clear recollection of the occasion, but perhaps my question triggered some process in his memory, because a few days later he was writing in the *Guardian* about the time he dropped an easy catch from Miller in front of the Ladies' Pavilion at Trent Bridge.

I walked on and watched one of the small boys buy a gas balloon for a gas balloon race. The girl didn't put enough gas in, so it drifted forlornly across the field at a height of around three foot. And a boy in a Texaco sun hat bowled his father with a leg break, and a very old woman sat eating her lunch on a bench dedicated to the memory of 'Lilian Ball who loved Gloucester County cricket and was Honorary Secretary of the Supporters Social Club from 5 November 1959 to 1970'. In the members' bar a girl, smiling grimly, asked an official, 'Are we all right for sandwiches – I've got to go and feed the band.' Outside the British Telecom Marquee a man contemplated an empty cardboard box and said, 'They get well looked after in there. Strawberries from bloody Kent. I'm a shareholder. I should be able to get in there.'

I went and sat down in the supporters club bar and had a pint. There was a picture of Jessop at the crease in a hooped cap about to pounce on a half-volley and another of Hammond – a copy of the famous one of him in his blazer. Someone ordered a pint of 'lunatic soup' and explained, 'Cider, that is'; another man came in and said, 'Who needs Lawrence with an Irishman like that Curran?' and the man behind the bar said, 'Trust 'e to say that.' Then someone else said, 'He's not Irish, his dad's from Ceylon and he's from Zimbabwe,' and the earlier speaker said, ''E's got an Irish passport, 'e wouldn't be playing for us if 'e wasn't Irish.' And someone else observed that if he had an Irish passport he must be eligible to play for England. They seemed rather pleased with their present team, and although the ghosts of everyone from Jessop and Hammond to Zaheer and Procter were invoked, they weren't just doing it to make invidious comparisons with the present. Perhaps they thought Procter really was a local lad and that Zaheer Abbas came from a Cotswold village of the same name.

Whatever his nationality Curran took five for 35 and the Australians were all out for 146. Then Gloucester lost six men while scoring only 122. It was hazy, hot and humid, and Gerry Turner, who was at the ground in 1948 when Australia made 774, went round selling raffle tickets and putting the money in a bucket. When I chatted to him in the secretary's office he said he supposed you could call him 'Mr Gloucester Cricket' because he'd not only watched practically every home game for years, he'd also been to every away ground apart from Trent Bridge. He used to play a bit for Chew Magna but his best games are billiards and snooker. Which reminded me that there is no pub by the ground, and the nearest, on the corner of Seymour and Nevil Roads, is called The Sportsman. It does not have a cricketer on its inn signs. On one there is a snooker player and on the other a darts player. This strikes me as very peculiar.

I dare say it was a very untypical day, but it was an interesting and exuberant one and the place was buzzing with noise and interest. Oddly enough I caught few echoes of the past, for despite Jessop's Tavern and Grace's Gates it does not strike one as a historic ground in the way that some do. I was disappointed not to see the Lord Mayor wearing his gold chain. But I was very pleased to come across a man by the pavilion wearing a blazer with an elephant's head on the breast pocket. Underneath the elephant it said 'Matabeleland'.

I like to think that you don't often see a Matabeleland cricket blazer at the Phoenix Assurance Ground at Bristol, but if so it only goes to show that I went on the wrong day. I should have chosen something more ordinary. All the same I shall always associate Bristol cricket ground with the day Gloucester bowled Australia out for 146 and the crowds came and the band played and the canvas billowed and I saw a man from Matabeleland by the pavilion.

OLD TRAFFORD

*'Hundreds of Lancashire
supporters weeping
into their mild and bitter'*

PLEASE DO NOT MOVE
WHEN THE BOWLING
IS FROM THIS END

WILSONS TRADITIONS

Very blue, Old Trafford.

This is not something that strikes those of us whose knowledge of the ground is second-hand. On television there are almost always bodies filling the seats, but on an overcast Lancashire day with the rain shafting in from the Pennines and the sawdust neatly piled at each end of the wicket the bodies are fairly few and far between. Even when the match in question is that classic of the English county championship, the Roses match itself. And when the seating is left exposed you can see that it's dark blue. Some of it is old bench seating and the paint is peeling. The new seats, however, are plastic bucket ones and the paint is bright. I had somehow always thought of Old Trafford as various shades of grey or maybe sepia. It was slightly shocking to find this venerable place's dignified monochrome so vividly slashed with colour.

'The Yorkshire match isn't what it was, I'm afraid,' Mr Warburton had warned me over the phone. He is the assistant secretary at Old Trafford and has been on the staff since 1947. The year before he joined, the first after the war, 37,091 souls had packed into the ground for the first day of the Roses match. Today we agreed there couldn't have been more than 1,500.

'It used to be four or five hundred runs a day in those days,' said an old codger in the stand to the right of the Wilsons stand – 'Wilsons. Traditional Brewers since 1834.' Wilsons put up the money for a covered way to run between the Ladies' Pavilion and the main, Gentlemen's one, but it didn't work out. However, they let Lancashire keep the money, provided they put the Wilsons sign up on the stand opposite the pavilion.

I mentioned the 1946 Roses match attendance to my friend, the senior spectator, and he grunted. Never mind thirty thousand plus for the First XI, he'd been at Old Trafford when there were twelve thousand to watch the Seconds. I expressed some surprise and asked him why he thought this was. 'Nowt else to do,' he said, propounding the view, quite frequently expressed around the cricket grounds of old England, that in the last thirty-odd years the quality of cricket has declined but the quality of life improved. It is not a universal view, but it is widely held.

Be that as it may, the cricket that morning was most diverting, mainly because of a young Jamaican called Balfour Patterson who bowled stunningly fast and accurately enough to clean bowl both Yorkshire openers (not Boycott, who was sadly absent) and finish the day with six for 77. Much later, when England went to the West Indies, Patterson was known to the cricket writers as 'Patrick' Patterson. I prefer Balfour. At one point when the players retired for drizzle

Yorkshire were 19 for three. Shortly after they went back they were 26 for four.

'It'll be over before they get yon covers on,' said one know-all on the pavilion steps, and he was right. It was one of those days when the weather seemed to be in a constant twitch of indecision. But it didn't worry Balfour, fresh from the Saddleworth League. The previous year, I was told, he was just as fast but he needed an umbrella of fine legs and third men to gather up the wide deliveries which eluded the keeper. This time he was bowling pretty straight and making it bounce disturbingly high. He made Paul Allott, who opened from the Warwick Road end, look quite ordinary.

It was sad the crowd was so small because it was obvious that the battle between Yorkshire and the Lancashire pace attack was being fought every inch of the way, and the ground, unlike others where there is a dearth of funds and or inclination, has been significantly modernised. Old Trafford was quite heavily bombed during the war. The Luftwaffe took the back off the Victorian pavilion and knocked down a stand or two, which was one reason why so many people got in for that 1946 Yorkshire game: they were standing, jammed tight, on the rubble.

Jerry ruined, jerry built. At least at first, for an early post-war vice-president had interests in corrugated asbestos, and you can still see a handful of corrugated asbestos roofs around to this day. The stand opposite the secretary's office was rebuilt in 1951 but was condemned as unsafe and has had to be replaced. The irony is that this short-lived stand was built by professional builders. Further round the ground another stand, not especially beautiful, is nevertheless an

effective memorial to the groundsman and four assistants who built it on their own with no outside assistance.

Latterly, however, the improvements appear more substantial. New stands, bucket seats, banqueting facilities, a restaurant open all the year round (the only place you can get a decent meal for miles except for the restaurant at Manchester United). It all brings in much needed cash as well. Of the twenty suites down by the old practice ground eighteen are let out for the whole year at around six thousand pounds a go while the other two are available for shorter 'lets'. There is a wonderful stained glass window in the foyer of these executive suites. It was presented to the great R. G. Barlow in the 1880s. All true Lancastrian cricket lovers revere Barlow. He took 726 wickets for Lancashire between 1871 and 1891, and 31 of them belonged to W. G. Grace. The window shows Barlow with the wicket-keeper Richard Pilling and Barlow's old skipper A. N. Hornby, and one can scarcely help recalling Francis Thompson's lines, hackneyed perhaps but still affecting:

> It is little I repair to the matches of the Southron folk,
>   Though my own red roses there may blow;
> It is little I repair to the matches of the Southron folk,
>   Though the red roses crest the caps, I know.
> For the field is full of shades as I near the shadowy coast,
> And a ghostly batsman plays to the bowling of a ghost,
> And I look through my tears on a soundless-clapping host
>   As the run-stealers flicker to and fro,
>   To and fro:–
> O my Hornby and my Barlow long ago.

Home thoughts from Lord's – a Lancashire version of Browning; words that, I suspect, will have hundreds of Lancashire supporters weeping into their Wilsons mild and bitter; and words you can't possibly omit from any consideration of Old Trafford. I wish I had had time to go to Blackpool to see Barlow's grave at Blackpool. Brian Bearshaw, who once lived in Blackpool and knew the headstone well, describes it as 'a large white stone showing a set of stumps with the ball passing through middle-and-leg, and at the bottom, three little words ... "Bowled at last".'

I expect it was sunnier at Old Trafford a hundred years ago when Hornby and Barlow were stealing their runs, and I am virtually certain poor depressed exiled Francis Thompson *thought* it was sunnier. I incline to the Hazare view. There is a letter from old Vijay at Old Trafford sent from his bungalow opposite the Polo Gymkhana in Baroda. It was written in response to an invitation sent out to lots of great cricketers a year or so ago to come and drink champagne and launch the Old Trafford Appeal for money for better buildings, 'Old Trafford,' wrote Hazare, 'seems to shine in the company of Jupiter

Pluvius. This combination makes batting a challenge. In 1946 I encountered such a wicket. I regard my score of 44 in the Old Trafford Test as one of my best. Pollard, the local hero (aptly red-haired), and Bedser proved a terror on this wicket. I hit the only six of my Test career in that innings.'

That is the sort of achievement the record books never notice. There are others in a similar category. Old Trafford was where Frank Tyson first played representative cricket – for Lancashire Second XI. It was where, in '56, Jim Laker took those nineteen Australian wickets. We all know about that. But how many of us realise that it was the first result in an England–Australia Old Trafford Test for fifty-one years? Denis Compton played what he considers his greatest Test innings here – '145 not out, including stitches' – against Australia in 1948. In the 1921 Test Armstrong contrived to bowl two overs in succession. But my favourite vignette is Gubby Allen's.

In 1934 he bowled the very first over in the Old Trafford Test and managed to make it last thirteen balls – six acceptable ones, three wides and four no-balls. (Two of the acceptable balls produced sharp, though missed chances at slip.) 'I recall this event,' wrote Allen, 'as my affection for Old Trafford stems from it. Instead of derision I received sympathy and humour from the members and public for which I shall always be grateful. One comment, entirely good-natured, still rings in my ears: "Ah skipper, take him off or he'll pass our total on his own." ' (England had declared at 617 for nine.)

As a southerner (though there seem to be more Healds round Manchester than anywhere else in England) I'm always faintly sceptical about the much vaunted northern sympathy and humour. Too often it involves a gratuitous rudeness under the pretext of calling spades spades, but Old Trafford really did seem friendly. In one almost deserted stand there were three small boys, sitting by the boundary fence. 'Ere we go, ere we go, ere we go!' they chanted every time a Yorkshire wicket fell. Every other over Graham Fowler came and fielded close by them. He was noticeably chatty and friendly, no question of being grand or stand-offish. Outside the pavilion the members seemed to stand more than at, say, Lord's and they ate and drank in a offhand fashion proscribed by MCC. One or two were dressed with quite flamboyant formality. One man had a red rose in his button-hole; another a brown bowler hat, exuberant whiskers and an orange-flowered bow-tie. But there were 'Guinness' T-shirts too, and evidently no nonsense about having to wear a collar and tie. I drank a pint of Wilsons in the huge bar at the back of the pavilion, the bit added on after the German bombing. Good beer, I thought. Several members lunched off it and plates of unaccompanied chips. One member pointed out another and said of him, 'Been a member thirty years, he has, and I've never seen him move from the bar.' It used, according to one friend of mine who used to work for the *Manchester Guardian*, to be rather an exclusive place. 'I couldn't have got in, in those days,' he said. 'Now anyone can become a member.'

Nevertheless there are proprieties still observed and traditions honoured. 'No bare torsoes please,' says one sign, nicely. And they still have a real live Ladies' Pavilion with a sign which says, 'Lady Subscribers may introduce one guest only.' Unaccompanied gentlemen are not allowed.

And they honour their own. Not just Paynter's sweater and J. T. Tyldesley's bat – almost black; and the scorecard of 1874 when an England XI played Twenty-Two of Rochdale or the 1935 photo of the Lancashire team which was the first ever to fly to an away match. The four modern office blocks hard by the practice ground have each been named after a Lancashire hero. There is Statham House and MacLaren and Duckworth and Washbrook, quite apart from Pilling and my Hornby and my Barlow in stained glass at the entrance to the executive suites. I wonder what they would have thought of 'executive suites'. I can't think Francis Thompson would have approved.

In an odd way I was pleased to see Old Trafford on a rather dour, grey, sparsely populated day. The cricket was keenly contested. Hartley and Bairstow staged a recovery, and then young Balfour came back with another three wickets and the White Rose lot were all out for 205. Lancashire got four overs in the dusk and Jarvis and Sidebottom took a wicket apiece. Honours even.

I took the train back to Manchester Piccadilly. A dingy little sub-urban line that passes within a six-hit of the ground, then threads through a modern industrial estate to the old Victorian inner city. Warwick Road is the cricket station. Old Trafford is further on. The train was almost as empty as the ground. I watched the weather trying to decide whether to rain and remembered the pantomime of players to-ing and fro-ing in and out of the pavilion; of the ground staff covering and uncovering the wicket. A mother and child got in at Deansgate. The boy was obviously a football hooligan of the future destined for the other, shriller, rougher Old Trafford. 'Stephen,' said his mother at last, 'Stop spitting out the window.'

A week later they played the first of the one-day internationals in Manchester. The sun shone. A capacity crowd of over twenty thou-sand. Bodies on every seat and not a hint of the bright blue bucket seats. A fine day's cricket; pint upon pint of Wilsons. And yet that's not my idea of Old Trafford. I cherish my day sitting with an old codger who could remember twelve thousand watching the Second XI and yet another West Indian fast bowler from the Saddleworth League bounding in past the little pyramid of sawdust. Vijay Hazare was right. Old Trafford shines in the company of Jupiter Pluvius.

NORTHAMPTON

*'W.G. arrived late
and was punched in
the face.
He never came again'*

Northamptonshire was my father's cricket love because he was brought up next door in Bedfordshire. His early heroes were men like Jupp and Timms, who were hardly of the class of Hammond or Hendren despite the 30,000 runs they scored between them. I, however, never went near the county in childhood and was unable to share his enthusiasm. This produced far and away the most acrimonious arguments of my childhood. Most of them, as I recall, centred around the performance of Raman Subba Row.

'Subba Row and Lightfoot put on 376 against Surrey.'

'375.'

'Six.'

'Five.'

Or even more ridiculous, 'Subba Row made 260 not out against Lancashire. It's the highest any Northants player has ever made.'

'Isn't.'

'Is.'

We never, as far as I can remember, argued about the finer points of the game; never discussed the aesthetic qualities of, say, Subba Row's cover drive as against that of Gimblett, or even whether Subba Row should play for England. It was always something statistical. And we never telephoned the *Daily Telegraph* information desk to arbitrate, just went on disagreeing until I was ordered to my room. I suspect a great many fathers and sons argue like this, which is why I now have a firm rule about arguments over certainties. 'Look it up,' I repeat boringly, no doubt irritating my children just as much as my father used to irritate me with his unquestioning advocacy of Northants in general and Subba Row in particular.

I had never even been to Northampton until July 1985 when they were playing Derbyshire. What I knew about the town would have taken up little more than the back of a postcard: boots and shoes; a football team unpromisingly called the Cobblers (as in 'What a load of ...') and the cricket. A quick cull through the reference books revealed that the town boasts one of England's only four round churches, and that Jerome K. Jerome, who wrote *Three Men in a Boat*, died suddenly in Northampton while on a motoring holiday in 1927. Not a lot else.

'Velkommen til Northampton,' said the sign outside the railway station, unexpectedly. On closer examination it turned out to be an advertisement for Carlsberg, who also sponsor the Northants cricketers. They have 'Carlsberg' on their sweaters. Everywhere, I reflected, is sponsorship. The committee acknowledge it in the annual report and duly list those companies which took advantage of the 'Hospitality

Lounge'. Carlsberg, of course, and the Northampton Development Corporation and Initial Automatic Services and Terry Wilson Laminates. There is a Betjeman poem waiting to be written here, beginning 'There's a breathless hush in the Hospitality Lounge. . . .'

The County Ground is the other side of town from the station, but it is worth the walk. I paused to investigate the 1160 Church of St Peter's, where the Greek Community of St Neophytos worship at noon every Sunday, and spent a few moments in All Saints'. All Saints' is a fine galleried seventeenth-century building with an imposing portico. Above it there is a very funny statue of Charles II dressed as a Roman in a sort of smock and thonged sandals. Here John Clare, the poet, who spent some years in the county lunatic asylum, used to come and sit. I have no idea if Clare was keen on cricket, but I like to think that he had the game in mind when he wrote, 'Summer's pleasures they are gone/Like to visions every one.'

There was a market in full swing in the market square with good-looking vegetables and a lot of naughty knickers at a stall marked 'Doug is here'. An elderly couple loaded down with plastic bags full of carrots and new potatoes gave me detailed and immaculate directions to the cricket, and I walked away from the centre, past the statue of Charles Bradlaugh, who was MP for Northampton, and down the Wellingborough Road. There was a lot of brick down the Wellingborough Road – a stark orange I associate with the Midlands and which I find rather depressing. There seemed to be a great many hairdressers, too. A policeman called me 'mate' when I asked if I was still going in the right direction; the cards in a newsagent's window said 'Second-hand Laura Ashley wedding dress ten pounds' and 'Young budgerigar with cage and accessories free to a good home'.

Almost at the gates of the ground is Manfield's shoe factory. I didn't know about Manfield's shoes, but the sign said 'Famous for Shoes'. They were looking for 'Experienced Closing Room Operatives, full and part time.' Then comes the Abington Park Hotel, a fine example of Northampton Baronial with an inn sign depicting the architect who designed it. He is M. H. Holding, and he has a look of H. G. Wells. I turned left along a vivid brick terrace of tiny cottages inaptly called Roseholme Road, and there were the gates. Northampton's gates are The C. J. T. Pool Gates. Pool played from 1905 to 1910, a useful bat who bowled a bit. There is a picture of him in the pavilion wearing a boater. At the gates there is a brief, dignified inscription under which someone had scrawled, 'Stuff the posers, i.e. Polly.'

This was by no means the earliest ground in the county. In 1741 the Gentlemen of Northamptonshire took on the Gentlemen of Buckinghamshire for twenty guineas a side on 'The Cow Meadow' outside town. It then became customary to fence off an area of the old racecourse but this doesn't seem to have been very satisfactory. The Freemen of the town complained that it was illegal to fence off the ground

and their complaints were upheld by the mayor, with the result that everyone climbed over the barricades and got in free. It all sounds rather chaotic. On one occasion W. G. Grace arrived late for a game and was punched in the face by an anonymous 'enthusiast'. It is said that the doctor never visited Northampton again.

Other, more sober 'enthusiasts', including the splendidly named Sir Herewald Wake, decided they must have somewhere more satisfactory to play, and in 1885 the Northants County Cricket and Recreation Ground Company Ltd was formed. At the same time it was 'proposed and carried that the offer of Mr Cockerill to fork, plough and seed the ground be accepted'. This was Alfred Cockerill, a self-made green-grocer of some resources. Over the years he seems to have taken on more and more responsibility for the ground, until in 1923, when the Company was wound up, Cockerill acquired the field and leased it back to the Trustees on a peppercorn rent for a thousand years.

In the pavilion there is a picture of Mr Cockerill holding a stout stick. He has a three-piece suit, a hat with an upturned brim almost like a stetson, a tie secured with a pin and amused, crinkly eyes. He looks rather pleased with himself, as well he might. The tribute underneath identifies him as the 'generous donor' of the grounds which are to be used 'in perpetuity for cricket and kindred sports'.

The 'kindred sports' rider accounts for some of the ground's peculiarity. Association Football is one, and bowls the other. This means that one corner, walled off, is a bowling green. No problem here. It also means that the end furthest from the pavilion and indoor school is taken up by Northampton Town's football club. For a startling, if short-lived period, the Cobblers were in the first division of the Football League, not something which Alfred Cockerill can have envisaged. Now they are back in the fourth, which is a more appropriate place for a club which shares its ground with a cricket club.

During cricket about two thirds of the football pitch is used as a car park. Behind the cars a grandstand full of new, empty plastic seats extends the full length of the ground. At each end there is old, rather dilapidated terracing. Up at the cricket end there is a new, rather hideous pavilion in yellow brick, a more elegant Victorian one, partly hidden by sightscreens, and between them an indoor school with seats and a press box on top. The press used to be in a very odd little building next to 'The Mound'. This looks like an Elizabethan signal box.

The only national newspaper with a correspondent in Northampton for the Derby match was the *Daily Telegraph*. They had sent the estimable Tony Winlaw, whom I first met in the hospitality tent on a cold foggy day in the Oxford Parks. Mr Winlaw dutifully introduced me to the oldest inhabitant, Fred Speakman, who has been reporting Northampton matches for forty years, mainly for the Press Association. Mr Speakman pointed out various features of the ground giving me the sort of inside information which only long association can produce. The top of the old pavilion, for instance, always used to be known as 'The Elephants' Cemetery' because that was where you went 'for a last bellyache' before you died. The West Stand was also famous for its 'grumblers', and at one stage there was a sort of revolving stand at the Football Ground end which was reversed at the beginning and end of every season.

At one point I moved round to sit near the vice-presidents in the bottom of the old pavilion and I was intrigued to hear that the grumbling was still going on.

'That was a bad ball!'

'Shocking!'

They did rather look as if they had set out that morning to have a jolly good grumble at the cricketers.

They had a point. Northampton declared at 219 for six, which meant that Derby had got to make 290 to win. They ended the day on 162 for six, and despite Williams's five for 34 I never thought there was the slightest chance of a result. Nor did the grumblers.

Over on the mound, however, there was less grumbling and some agreeable nostalgia when the distinctive white thatch of the recently retired D. S. Steele, Northants and England, came and sat down behind me with a friend. He was very appreciative of everything and, of course, knowledgeable as well. Not just about the cricket: 'Well you've got two back foot players, haven't you?' but also such essentials as the catering. The food is very good in the pavilion dining-room these days. It's not so long ago that the players and spectators all trooped over to the County Tavern just outside the football ground end. It was good to see David Steele acepting the respectful greetings of spectators and being awarded the best table in the dining-room. Cricketing prowess induces a very particular sort of hero worship. Like the game itself it is friendly and unfrenzied. At Northampton you sensed the crowd giving itself a collective nudge and a wink as they saw him coming. 'One of the last, if not the last, of the old-fashioned professionals,' says the club's official tribute. He scored over 18,000 runs and took more than 450 wickets in first-class cricket for Northants and no one who was watching cricket in 1975 will ever forget the way he performed after being pitched into an ailing Test side. Definitely worth a verse of Henry Newbolt.

As he left the ground he called out to someone on the mound seating: 'If Virg turns up, tell him he's opening.' The reference was clearly to Roy Virgin of Somerset and Northants, but I couldn't take it further than that. Odd though how cricket seems so riddled with nicknames.

You couldn't call Northampton a beautiful ground. The ugly pavilion, the Tudor signal box, the long plastic slash of football ground stand, red brick houses and their back gardens. But it does have two churches within sight and this always improves a cricket ground. One is moderately nondescript, but the other, St Matthew's, is a real oddity. Situated over by the old racecourse, it is a large Victorian building with a long cricket tradition of its own. The choir fielded a team before the present church was built. (Its predecessor was a temporary iron structure opened on Palm Sunday 1895 and built at a cost of £603 14s 3d.) The choir won its first match by six runs – outscoring Great Houghton by 48 to 42. The present church was built with money from Phipps the brewers in memory of Pickering Phipps who, like Bradlaugh, was once Northampton's MP. And the architect was none other than Matthew Holding, the H. G. Wells look-alike who was responsible for the Abington Park Hotel on the other side of the cricket ground.

But the glory of St Matthew's really dates from the appointment of Walter Hussey as vicar in 1937. For the fiftieth anniversary of the church's consecration Hussey staged a festival for which he commissioned a piece by Benjamin Britten, 'Rejoice in the Lamb', and a statue, 'Madonna and Child', by Henry Moore. It is still there and definitely worth a detour. Opposite it in the south transept there is a Graham Sutherland crucifixion, also specially commissioned. Apart from Britten's contribution, Tippett, Lennox Berkeley, Malcolm Arnold, Richard Rodney Bennett and others have all written special music for the church and there is a St Matthew's Day Litany and Anthem by Auden. Even if, when you visit the county ground at Northampton, you do not also go to St Matthew's, it is refreshing to be able to look at the spire in the distance and reflect on the extraordinary art it has fostered since the 1940s.

For the most part the ground is a more prosaic affair. There is a 1929 team pictured in the pavilion which sums up the essentially stolid nature of Northampton cricket. Recite this list out loud and see what I mean (especially if you can imitate John Arlott's voice): Bakewell, Partridge, Clark, L. Bullimer (scorer), Liddell, Thomas, Matthews, Cox, Woolley, V. W. C. Jupp, Bellamy, Timms. That is a list which goes well with the note from the 1891 minutes which says, 'It was resolved that the application of the lady cricketers be not entertained, which was carried unanimously.'

Northampton has had its lighter moments too, provided by the likes of Tyson, Milburn, and F. R. Brown. And it was here that Percy Fender scored a century in thirty-five minutes.

For me, however, its physical presence can never match the memory of those childhood clashes over Subba Row's batting average or George Tribe's bowling figures. As I sat in the stand above the cricket school, I watched one of that strange band of statistical cricketing fanatics entering each ball into his scorebook ... dot, dot, dot. To him the accurate recording of each moment of the day mattered terribly, just as it used to matter so very much to me and my father that Subba Row scored 7,050 runs in 186 innings at an average of 43.79 precisely.

I do hope there is a complete set of *Wisden* in the library wherever he has gone.

ARUNDEL

*'Visitors are requested
to speak quietly
and behave reverently'*

In 1895 Henry Fitzalan-Howard, fourteenth Duke of Norfolk, hired two hundred out-of-work labourers, equipped them with picks, shovels, wheelbarrows, axes and saws, and sent them off into the woods near his castle at Arundel. He wanted a cricket ground. When he asked what was the biggest cricket ground in England he was told that it was the Kennington Oval. 'Make mine the same size,' he told his men. And so they did, and the result is an amphitheatre of great beauty, one of the most beautiful cricket grounds anywhere in the world. They told me at Arundel that when C. B. Fry was walking round the ground with Bernard, the fifteenth Duke, C.B., who was a notorious polymath, remarked casually that he had identified thirty-two different varieties of tree. My impression is that C.B. was also a fearful show-off because he then named each variety, in both English and Latin. Duke Bernard wore a little learning lightly and was not, in my experience, one of the world's great listeners. Being one of the world's great cricket enthusiasts, however, I suppose he let C.B. bang on about the trees because of his heroic qualities as a cricketer.

Although the ground was built by the fourteenth Duke, it is the fifteenth Duke's memory that haunts it. He played there practically all his life, and his widow Lavinia is now the president of the Arundel Castle Cricket Club, 'thereby', as she puts it, 'helping the sport that was so dear to my husband's heart'. It was he who instituted the tradition whereby the foreign touring teams always begin their season with a game at Arundel. And he who insisted that cricket at Arundel should always be positive. It was not done in his day to draw matches. Ronnie Ford, now chairman of the club, told me that when his son first played at Arundel he batted in a tentative style best described as 'puddingy'. Coming in at lunch he found Duke Bernard standing in front of the pavilion. 'Young man,' he said sternly, 'if you go on batting like that you will never play at Arundel again.'

The editor of this book accompanied me to Arundel wearing a straw hat of some distinction. It was in the Panama style but came from the South of France. Real Panama hats, my researches suggest, originally came from Ecuador, so they are not strictly speaking Panama hats at all. Proper Ecuador hats are made from the underdeveloped leaves of the stemless screw pine or jipijapa (*Carludovica palmata*) and really proper Ecuadors have I Zingari ribbons round them. My editor's hat had no ribbon but was still a very acceptable cricket-watching hat. When I saw it I mentally promised myself something similar as a reward for finishing the book, though I am not sure about wearing one without an IZ ribbon and I am no more likely to be made a member of the IZ than of the Athenaeum or the Grand Order of Water Rats.

His was the only straw hat on view that morning. This surprised me. I had imagined a veritable crocodile of elderly chaps in Panamas or Ecuadors striding towards the cricket. The cricket wasn't even signposted. There was a notice saying, 'British Doll Artists Exhibition', and a plethora of shoppe signs in Gothick. Arundel is a little too pretty for its own good and is plainly on the tourist track. I suspected this the minute I saw all the Gothick script, and my suspicions were confirmed when I saw a sign in a shop window printed by the Sussex police. It said, 'Persons caught stealing will be arrested' and it was in ten different languages. Bloody foreigners!

Arundel is very obviously Norfolk-in-Sussex. The main hostelry is the Norfolk Arms and on a wall on the other side of the street is a memorial to Duke Bernard, who was not only Duke but also Mayor of the town in 1935–36. Not many towns can have had a mayor who was also the Earl Marshal of England. It is also very obviously a pocket of Roman Catholicism. The Anglican church (closed and locked) is quite modest, but the Catholic one is a great soaring nonsense. It is a pastiche of a French cathedral of around 1400 commissioned by the fifteenth Duke in 1868 and designed by Joseph Hansom, the man who invented the cab. He also did Birmingham Town Hall. In 1965 it was elevated from being a mere church to a fully fledged cathedral, and in 1971 the remains of the family saint, St Philip Howard, were transferred to a custom-built shrine in the north transept. St Philip, not to be confused with his namesake the Literary Editor of *The Times*, a forceful if myopic bat and occasional Eton Rambler, was sentenced to death by Elizabeth I and died under mysterious circumstances (poison?) at the age of thirty-nine after eleven years' imprisonment.

There was a flower festival going on: beautiful arrangements all round the church and a quartered banner made entirely of petals laid out on the floor at the foot of St Philip's shrine. I particularly liked the notice which said: 'Visitors are requested to speak quietly and behave reverently.' An even better text, thought my editor, for a cricket ground than a church.

The cathedral is the only building visible from the cricket ground, though that is not the view you usually see in the postcards. The cricket ground, being high up, is not visible from the cathedral, so we had to ask the way from one of the flower ladies. She replied, surprisingly, 'Which ground?'. Apparently there is a town ground which, she seemed to be implying, was just as famous in Arundel as the la-de-da ground up by the castle. Still there were no signs to the cricket, indeed what signs there were deterred rather than encouraged. 'No dogs, motor cars or motor cycles are allowed,' said the one at the park entrance; and further on we found 'Caution Rifle Range: Keep out of Danger Area shown by notice boards when red flags are flown.' Then, when at last there was a sign saying simply, 'Cricket', there was a sister sign saying 'Caution racehorses'. What is more, a dangerously skittish racehorse hove in sight at just that moment and seemed on the point of bolting when a car, driven by an elderly 'Friend of Arundel Cricket Club' rounded the bend.

Then suddenly it was there: a great green amphitheatre with stumps already in place. One or two cars were parked around the boundary, and four hundred scarlet plastic seats were stacked at intervals, though most were in front of the pavilion. 'I know a cafeteria in the Forest of Dean just like that,' said my editor, lugubriously, and I saw what he meant. Until 1965 the pavilion was a tent. The Duke's guests changed up at the big house. A tent was all you needed at the ground. Not until the sixties did they think there was any need for a permanent building actually at the site of the cricket. The sixties was not a very inspired period in cricket pavilion architecture. No thatch, no veranda, no baroque belfry nor gilded weathervane, just a functional brown timber building with a high tiled roof.

Until recently the office was a caravan, but now it too is a permanent affair. In a sense it is a cricketing equivalent of the House of Lords. A House of Lord's perhaps. When I looked in I found Ronnie Aird, former secretary and president of MCC, and the club chairman Ronnie Ford, a former assistant secretary of MCC, and the club secretary, Veronica Lloyd, who also used to work at Lord's, as Ronnie Ford's assistant. Earlier in the week I had spoken to S. C. 'Billy' Griffith, another ex-assistant secretary of MCC and recently retired as chairman of Arundel. I had hoped to see him at Arundel but he was, sadly, unable to be there, his mobility much restricted by a long debilitating illness.

These Lord's emeriti, together with Colin Cowdrey, Eddie Harrison, the Hon. Sec. of the Sussex Martlets, and the Duchess herself, are the people who have kept cricket going at Arundel in the manner that Duke Bernard would have wished. When he died in 1975, the title and the castle passed to his cousin, a career soldier of sixty who had never lived at Arundel and had little discernible interest in cricket. Lavinia, the Dowager Duchess, was determined that the cricket should continue and convened this select group of old bold cricketing folk to make sure it did.

The plan was to form a non-playing membership and to bolster the money from their subscriptions with sponsorship wherever possible. The scoreboard, for instance, was presented by Benson and Hedges. In 1985 there were just under two thousand members entitled to the dark blue club tie with its single red 'N' motif. Each member pays ten pounds a year, a husband and wife fifteen. There is a hard core of three or four hundred locals and the rest are scattered worldwide.

For this particular game - Lavina Duchess of Norfolk's XI against the Barbados Wanderers - there was a tiny scattering of spectators, their cars ranged around the ground while they sat alongside mainly

in their own deck chairs (the present policy is to encourage people to bring their own seats!). The weather was iffy and it was mid-week so this was hardly surprising. Normally they would expect a couple of hundred. For the annual match against the foreign tourists several thousand turn up, stretching Arundel's slim resources and demanding all the canniness and experience built up during those years at cricket HQ.

All in all Arundel puts on over forty games a year, ranging from such serious stuff as the Duchess's XI against the Australians, Ireland or Combined Services, through the Martlets' games where the opponents would be such teams as Free Foresters, Kenya Kongonis or Hampshire Hogs, to the Estate XI which plays village cricket.

Over in the pavilion Ronnie Ford bought pints all round and showed off some of the pictures of great moments in Arundel's past. The George Cox benefit in 1951 with a photograph of G. H. G. Doggart, Gubby Allen and the Duke. The famous Duke of Edinburgh's XI versus Duke of Norfolk's XI in 1953 when Edinburgh clean bowled Norfolk and 25,000 people came to cheer. There is a photo of Prince Charles when he came with his team from HMS *Norfolk*, and a

Lawrence Toynbee painting of the Duke padded up and looking quizzically bellicose, the artist just behind. Like so many pavilions, Arundel has its own poem. This one, composed in 1936 by Peter Wood, begins:

> Beneath the stately Dukely trees
> His Grace's peasants on their knees ...

and ends:

> The rest all cried 'A batsman true!'
> But then the Duke had told them to.

Lunch was delicious quiches and salads and raspberry pudding, with players down one end of the pavilion and members at the other. Then it rained, and the players stood and gazed out at the grey and one couldn't help wondering why West Indians should bother to come all this way to be rained on. The Barbados captain was P. D. B. Short, a sprightly 59-year-old who had been Chairman of the West Indies Board of Control and had the most wonderful white Jimmy Edwards moustaches.

As there was no play I settled down with the old scorebooks. Wonderful reading for a wet afternoon. One or two of the old matches were in beautiful copperplate which must, thought today's two scorers, Karen Marshall and Elizabeth Bisset, have been copied in after the event. Too perfect otherwise. Every match shows Duke Bernard, identified simply as 'His Grace'. His abilities never matched his enthusiasm, poor fellow. Time and again he is out in single figures or bowls without a wicket. Still, neither Len Hutton nor F. S. Jackson troubled the scorers when they came. The real heroes of the pre-war years were men like the Crawleys, Aidan and Cosmo; Alec Douglas-Home, then Lord Dunglass; and J. C. Masterman, author of one of the best of all Oxford novels, Provost of Worcester College, a mandarin figure who I remembered interviewing me for a scholarship and deploying half-moon glasses to terrifying effect. The pages reeked of creamy flannels and Harlequin caps. Major Staniforth's XI; Captain Hope's XI; Lord Eldon's XI; His Grace's XI versus the 3rd Battalion, the Grenadier Guards. The Duke must have enjoyed the time his team beat a Sussex XI by one wicket at 6.30. He got a wicket, too. Every time a 'palpable catch' was dropped it was recorded with a 'c' in the batsman's score and the bowler's analysis. Not many palpable catches the day Aidan Crawley made 147 in 55 minutes against Lord Eldon's XI. Nor next day when he made 164 in 77. The names! Mr Maxwell Scott, Captain Disney Roebuck and Mr De la Bere, all of whom played in Colonel FitzClarence's XI.

And His Grace, fielding, always, at mid-off.

The second the rain stopped the players were back on the field. No nonsense here about bad light or a slippery outfield. From the pavilion the ground looked a picture – a sylvan oval with not a building in sight. (There are loos out there, ugly corrugated iron ones, but they are hidden away in the rhododendrons.) Just opposite there is a cut in the trees, ordered by Duke Bernard, who felt that the ground was too enclosed and claustrophobic. The view stretches away across the flat plain of the Arun valley to the Downs beyond. It is a master's touch, the final flourish of the brush.

I never saw the fifteenth Duke play cricket, but as a reporter I watched him mastermind the Investiture of the Prince of Wales at Caernarvon. He did behave preposterously at times. I remember Nick Tomalin at a press conference once calling out from the back, 'Could you speak up? We can't hear what you're saying.'

'Well,' riposted the Duke, 'I can't hear you either.'

The press corps found him amusing, not always intentionally, but I don't remember anyone disliking him, and his sense of style and his eye for detail were unsurpassed. Both are apparent at the Arundel ground, a singularly beautiful place and an apt memorial. The traditional convention always was that His Grace got one free run. Once, the town's fast bowler, a local coal heaver, forgot the rule and bowled him for nought. The Duke thought it as funny as anyone, but if there is a lingering wistfulness about Arundel and His Grace's ghostly presence it is a slight sadness that he so seldom managed better than the forlorn entry: 'His Grace ... b. Captain Foster 1.'

GRACE ROAD, LEICESTER

'Jack used to work down the mine at Bagworth Colliery'

'Not easily accessible to the casual spectator,' wrote Yardley and Kilburn about Leicester's Grace Road ground just after the war, and it has become no more accessible in the intervening years. For a long time the county played at the Aylestone Road ground, much nearer the city centre, but this was severely blighted when the local electricity works was built next door. Black gritty dust fell all over the ground, making flannels grimy and ruining Norman Yardley's egg and tomato sandwiches; and the cooling towers, which have now been blown up, made everything impossibly damp. During the war the Germans dropped a couple of bombs on the main stand. Leicester have only played three games there since the war – two in 1957 against Hampshire and Derby, and one in 1962 against Cambridge University.

You pass this ground, with its timbered Victorian pavilion, on your way up to the county's present home. It is a long trek on foot from the centre of town, and the citizenry of Leicester were very hazy about how to get there. So it took me some time to get my bearings. One old codger even tried to get me to go to the old Aylestone Road ground, where I would have been lucky to see anything more exotic than the Leicester Electricity Sports and Social Club versus Narborough and Littlethorpe or Broughton Astley.

It was my first joint excursion with Paul Cox, the illustrator, and it was interesting to go with someone who had studied architecture and had a trained eye. 'Blood and bandage,' he said, eyeing the Victorian extravagance of the Grand Hotel. 'Blood and bandage' is the 'in' phrase for that mixture of red brick and whiteish stone which you often get in Victorian municipal building.

In the end we discovered that the best way to the cricket was a 36 or 37 bus. We had walked in the wrong direction, taking in a busy covered market outside the Corn Exchange. This is ducal country. The streets are named Belvoir and Rutland and Granby and there is a statue of John Henry, Duke of Rutland, which alleges that 'the inhabitants of the county and town of Leicester during the 50th anniversary of his high office with universal consent caused this statue to be erected.' A likely story!

The cricket ground used to be owned by the Dukes of Rutland but was bought from them in 1878. The family does not seem to have been closely connected with cricket since then except for a year in the thirties when the ninth Duke was president of the club. The present Duke does not appear to be much of a cricketer, though he is a considerable local figure.

The 36 passes along all the ducal streets, past the statue of John Biggs, an obviously eminent Victorian unknown to me, past Jokers

Wine Bar and the Bricklayers Arms and the Mazid Tandoori Take Away and the gaol which looks like a child's fort and the skating rink and the Granby Halls and the Leicester Football Club where the 'Tigers' play rugby. Shortly after a small field full of geese by the side of a canal our bus stopped and a woman passenger came upstairs and said, 'If you want the cricket you get off here.'

There was no sign of cricket. The house opposite the stop said 'Knighton Fields Infant School – Nursery Annexe', and we headed left until we saw the Lancashire team coach in the car park of an Everards pub called The Cricketers. Getting warm.

It was not a very attractive area. Small, rather mean terraced houses and drab factories and warehouses; 'Glenfield Marketing: Importers and Wholesalers for the Pet and Aquatic Trades' – did they deal in goldfish? On the corner of Grace and Millington Streets you could get 'Hot and Cold Cobs' from a cafe called 'The Rumbling Tum'. A man in J and P Coats (UK) Ltd asked if we were interested in making a purchase.

Lancashire were batting by the time we got into the ground. They faced a total of 327. It was the first day of the Old Trafford Test, so Leicester were without Gower and Agnew while Lancashire were missing Allott. One extra Leicester man on the field was Jack Birkenshaw, who scored more than 10,000 runs and took over 900 wickets for the county.

Today he was back on home turf, umpiring in a white coat. Leicester has been a fertile nursery for first-class umpires, though oddly enough it is not necessarily the best players who make the most successful umpires. Dickie Bird, for example, probably the best known of all contemporary umpires, played for Leicester from 1960 to 1964. He scored a thousand runs in his first season but declined after that, ending with an average of only 19.21. His fellow Test umpire, David Constant, averaged just over twenty. Though he played less often than Bird, he did get a wicket – one for 36. Bird got nought for 22. Nobody at Leicester passed any comment on Bird as a player, but one man did venture of Constant: 'Opening bat; slow, but useful to have around.'

But the most successful transformation from moderate Leicester player is that of F. M. Turner. Between 1954 and 1959 Turner had sixteen innings, scoring 196 runs for an average of 17.82. And he took three wickets for 223 with his leg spin bowling. As John Arlott has said, 'He simply did not make the grade as a player.' But in 1985 Mike Turner celebrated twenty-five years as secretary of the Leicestershire County Cricket Club. The successful modern club and the exceedingly well-appointed modern ground are very much Mike Turner's babies.

It is not a beautiful ground. From the seating above the pavilion block you can see the city of Leicester in the distance, but from ground level the only visible buildings are rows of terraced houses and their back gardens. There used to be forty-eight great elms along two sides

of the ground, but they were felled at the time of the Dutch elm disease. 'All mature,' says Mike Turner, wistfully, 'and we lost the lot.' The whitebeam and lime which replaced them are not yet a real substitute. At the car park end there are silver birches and mountain ash planted fifteen years ago. By the public lavatories there is a single weeping willow.

I entered by the George Geary stand, named after the great Leicester bowler who played from 1912 to 1938. The pavilion block is to the right. It has all been built since 1965, when the county bought the ground from the local education authority. The pavilion itself was opened on 25 June 1966 by the Lord Bishop of Leicester, who began his speech with the words 'Pavilion'd in splendour. . . .'

Compared with the old days it is indeed splendid. Jim Laker, the Surrey and England spinner, has recalled the old Grace Road in a little essay called 'The Good Old Days'. The title is ironic. Describing a visit to the ground, he wrote that 'it looked its usual broken-down shambles and it seemed quite incredible that those rickety, worn-out old steps which led into darkness to the leaky, spasmodic cold shower had not yet completely disintegrated. The changing-rooms remained indescribable.'

Today the facilities at Grace Road are by common consent the best in county cricket, apart from the Test grounds. In fact there was one year when it looked as if Leicester was going to stage a one-day international but, much to Mike Taylor's chagrin, the Test and County Cricket Board changed its mind.

Modern functionalism has meant few frills. The old weathervane with its ubiquitous flying fox is still there, and there are two flagpoles for the county standards. Otherwise it is simply a series of rectangles with plastic seats on top. The only odd building is the one they call 'The Meet'. (You get the impression at Leicester that the only permissible pastime other than cricket is fox-hunting.) There is pub food and drink in the Meet, a good view from the big glass windows, but it looks like a Nissen hut and was described by one spectator as 'a temporary structure that seems to have become permanent'.

In contrast to the contemporary austerity of the pavilion and executive suites there were deck chairs on hire at 25p a day. And flower-beds ringed the pavilion end of the ground, filled with roses. In the summer of '84, I was told by one of the older inhabitants, some people scattered tomato seeds among the roses and were putting the fruits in their sandwiches in August.

Just by the Meet I came across the secretary of the Enderby club, David Brown. Mr Brown hails from Lancashire, which is why every year when Lancashire are the visitors he takes three days off from his job with the Gas Board down the Aylestone Road. It was he who showed me the members' bar and the dining-room, where they were offering a lunch of roast lamb and raspberries for five pounds a head, and recalled Hallam and Inman and the Indian summer of Tony Lock. Leicester have made quite a speciality of Indian summers. Lock performed prodigies for them after his career with Surrey had come to an end; Willie Watson made two thousand runs in a season after Yorkshire dispensed with his services; best of all, another Yorkshire reject, Ray Illingworth, captained the county to victory in two Benson and Hedges Cups, two John Player Leagues, and in 1975 the championship itself. That was the first time Leicester had pulled of the championship. All the victory pennants hang in the committee room next to Mike Turner's office, along with the flag commemorating a Leicester game against I Zingari in 1850.

In the best tradition of all cricket fans of a certain age, Mr Brown lamented the good old days when 'You had eleven or twelve hundred runs scored and still got a result at the end of the day' and when 'we had an old-style pub and an old-style landlord and the lads would come in and have toasted sandwiches and a few beers.' He was also a little dubious about Mike Turner being awarded a club benefit. Mr Brown narrowed his eyes and wondered whether, despite Mr Turner's manifest good deeds, this didn't create a dangerous precedent.

I counted three stuffed foxes in glass cases around the ground and I dare say I missed a few. Their other souvenirs are more conventional. They have a good collection of caps, including some lovely old Leicestershire county caps – blue and maroon hoops from 1921 to 1929;

blue, white and gold hoops in 1930. Much better than the plain modern ones. Also Lord Crawshaw's Eton Rambler Cap. And George Geary's cap and boots, the first boots I'd seen at a county ground. Very stout workaday boots with never a hint of an Adidas label. And there is the ball he bowled with when taking ten Glamorgan wickets for eighteen at Pontypridd. The Leicestershire blazer belonged to J. Shields, who batted 209 times for the county between 1906 and 1923 but only scored 1,307 runs for an average of just over eight. Not much of a bowler either. Nought for four. There is a flier for a county cricket bazaar at The Temperance Hall, and another announcing the contest between Twenty-Two of Leicester and an England XI which included Barlow and Hornby. And lots of Leicester ties: the Quorn Hunt farmers, the Grace Road Taverners and the Gentlemen of Leicester, and Hinckley Town and Mountsorrel Castle. One of the photographs shows Ray Illingworth presenting a sheepish-looking David Gower with his county cap after he had carried his bat for 135 against Warwick on Sunday 28 August 1977.

Outside by the roses Paul Cox was sketching two veteran stalwarts of the Ibstock Town cricket club, Jack Walker and Bill Ottey. Jack captained the second eleven; Bill used to go in number eleven for the first. He seldom got an innings because they were a bit good. One time they scored 492 for seven declared.

Jack used to work down the mine at the Bagworth colliery with Les Taylor, the fast bowler, and with his father.

'You know Les's breakfast the other day?' he asked. 'A pork pie, packet of crisps, and a pint of beer.' They chortled, and then told me how a friend of theirs called Don Smith had been sitting by the sight-screen at the car park end when Keith Miller was batting for Australia. Apparently Miller hit a straight six and the ball bounced off the sight-screen and hit their friend Don on the head. They very much approved of Miller. They remembered one time when he caught the ball and then put it in his pocket. And another when he hid it in the pile of sawdust at the bowler's end. And then there was the man in the Ibstock side who was hit in the box rather painfully, and while he was recovering one of the fielding side picked up his bat and hid it up his trouser leg. 'Oh those were the things that made cricket characters,' they said, bemoaning the lacklustre professionalism of the modern game.

When Paul finished his picture they examined it with approval and some surprise.

'It's quite good, in't it?'

'I think 'e's made me look a bit better than usual.'

'Shall you autograph it?'

I couldn't help feeling that there were worse ways of spending your retirement than sitting by the roses and watching your old mining colleague bowling fast at Graham Fowler. Though it would have been

nice if it had been sunnier and less windy. Of course it had been better in the old days, they all said that, but give Mr Turner his due, this was the only ground in England where the players had to wear their blazers in the dining-room and you couldn't bring your dog. At other places the members' dogs peed on the pitch and even fouled the wicket. I remembered Swansea where the *Telegraph* correspondent's dog had been sick in the press box. It couldn't happen at Grace Road.

The artist and I lunched in the top of the Meet. Scotch egg and a respectable pint of Everards 'Tiger' beer. Then I went and talked to the impressive Mike Turner about his benefit and his plans for the future. He is hoping for a million pounds' worth of sports complex. At the moment the indoor cricket school doubles as the dining-room in summer. Most importantly, Mr Turner wants a sports clinic. No one in the city specialises in sports injuries and he wants to change that. We watched the Leicester cricket through the window and Old Trafford on the television, and I noticed that whereas some secretaries say 'they' are going to do so and so, and others say 'we' are going to do so and so, Mr Taylor said 'I' am going to do so and so. Judging by the eulogies from the great and good of cricket in his 'Mike Turner Testimonial Brochure', he is entitled to. Indeed, if he didn't, I doubt that Grace Road would have undergone the transformation it plainly has. Still, I couldn't help noticing.

Outside, batting was a struggle for everyone but a loping, stooping, bespectacled figure who scored a century while all about him fell. It was Clive Lloyd playing only his third county match that season. One of the joys of serendipitous cricket watching is the sudden unexpected treat. He made 131 before Taylor, yet to be picked for England and the West Indian tour, had him caught by Clift. The next highest score was 41. Despite his advancing years, and a bespectacled stoop which makes him appear even older, he still looked more than a class above any other batsman.

The artist and I took the bus back to the city centre but stopped for a brief act of pilgrimage at the old Aylestone Road ground, where the smuts used to get in the sandwiches and the cooling towers made the ball swing unplayably. One of the old gatemen at Grace Road had told me how he used to go and watch cricket there in the thirties and how there was always a band at tea-time, and how the amateurs and gentlemen left the pavilion from opposite ends of the building and met up half-way to the wicket and how Hobbs and Sutcliffe ... and how '... it was more sort of entertaining then.'

The black-and-white Victorian pavilion is vast and empty and decayed. Upstairs we found the secretary of the Leicester Electricity Sports and Social Club. He showed us the original architect's drawings for the pavilion. It would have been a great high-roofed Victorian monster, but undeniably grand. The present relic has a flat roof, but the secretary could not tell us whether it had ever been different.

It felt sad. I remembered Shields's blazer and Geary's boots and those wonderful hooped county hats of the twenties and thirties. It was here that Leicester scored 557 for four declared against New Zealand – and were all out for 26 against Kent. They bowled York-shire out for 47 one day at Aylestone Road; and it was here that Coe made 252 not out the year the Great War began; and here that George Geary and Alec Skelding once put on 96 for the last wicket against Kent. The contrast with the modern bustle of Grace Road is quite eerie. This place feels almost haunted. In fact I like to think that on a moonlit night, if you happened to be in the pavilion at Aylestone Road, you might just hear George Geary's boots as they clattered down the steps and out across the grass, speckled once again from the smutty snow from the electricity works next door. The present and the future is at Grace Road all right. But much of the past is here.

TORRY HILL

'Rain stopped play'

There are still a few private gentlemen's cricket grounds in England – the sort of place where you would expect to find R. C. Robertson-Glasgow explaining that 'on the Saturday we always play Colonel Cochrane's XI', or speculating on the form of the local vicar.

One of the best known is at Torry Hill, near Sittingbourne in Kent, where Robin Leigh-Pemberton, Governor of the Bank of England, stages a few games every summer, perpetuating a tradition begun in the mid-nineteenth century when the first ever match of the Band of Brothers, the Kentish touring club, was held on the lawn in front of the family house. The Leigh-Pembertons made up half the founding membership, and even now the family can field a formidable combination if the Governor himself can be persuaded to put on his wicket-keeping pads.

I felt it was indicative of a proper sense of priorities when Mr Leigh-Pemberton agreed to talk cricket at the Bank one Monday afternoon. An audience with the Governor is rather like one with royalty. To start with you are handed, like a baton, from one flunkey to another in a relay that takes you along interminable corridors of power. These flunkeys have tail coats of a strawberry ice cream colour that seems too flamboyantly Cecil Beaton to be entirely authentic.

The actual introduction follows royal convention, too. With ordinary nobs you are ushered into their office; they rise; come out from behind their desk and shake your hand. Royalty and the Governor of the Bank of England cause you to be flunkeyed into an ante-room, then themselves enter the ante-room, greet you and conduct you into their inner sanctuary. Or something like that. The point seems to be that they must be the person doing the entering, not you.

His father, he said, laid down the ground in the thirties but it was used mainly by the village. It was the headquarters of the Torry Hill

Cricket Club, but the village is very tiny and the ground is a mile away from it. There is not much scope for diversion for wives and children – not even a pub. Gradually the village players drifted away to other local clubs around Sittingbourne, until finally Torry Hill CC folded. The Leigh-Pembertons were determined to keep the ground up, however, and since then it has reverted to being a private country house ground.

As such its games are predominantly for what the old pros would call 'fancy caps'. I Zingari, Band of Brothers, Harlequins, Eton Ramblers, Arabs – these are the sort of clubs that perform at Torry Hill. At the end of Canterbury Cricket Week Mr Leigh-Pemberton's XI play the Old Stagers, who put on plays in the town all week. 'That's a bit of a mob game,' says the Governor. 'My sons and one or two of the oldest inhabitants. We do have men in their seventies who are quite capable of bowling a few people out.' Each of the half-dozen wickets is used a couple of times a year, and the head groundsman is the Leigh-Pembertons' retired gardener Mr Trinder.

It sounds idyllic. The surroundings are pastoral. The directions read rather like the ones John le Carré once gave me for his Cornish house. You pass twice over the motorway, right at the war memorial, left between the church and post office, right at the cedar, watch out for the ducks on the road at Bredgar, park by the clock tower. After following directions like these you expect to find George Smiley, standing enigmatically in the shadow of the pavilion, dressed perhaps in an umpire's coat or dozing dangerously in a deck chair.

I chose the wrong day.

The Governor's team was playing I Zingari on the first Sunday in August, and the first Sunday in August was like the first day of the great flood. I could see through the sheeting rain that the Kent countryside must be very beautiful round Torry Hill. I parked by the clock tower and squelched up the track to the deserted cricket field. The pavilion was shut and empty, though when I peered through a window I saw an empty champagne bottle and two glasses, and thought again of Smiley. Someone had left a smart cricket bag covered in labels. But there was no sign of life. Behind the pavilion there lurked a Barford motor roller with 'Big Bertha' written on her side.

I walked out to inspect Mr Trinder's wicket. Even the pile of sawdust at the bowler's end was wet through and the consistency of porridge. When I pressed my toe into the wicket the water covered my shoe. They do not appear to have covers at Torry Hill, and the water was running into the stump holes and forming a puddle around the popping crease. The clumps of beeches around the field swayed and dripped and the low clouds scudded towards the coach house, from which there emanated the hum of conversation as frustrated cricketers took an early lunch at the Governor's trestle tables.

It was the same all over England. Rain stopped play.

RAMSBOTTOM

'An immediate
and vivid image of
a Bill Tidy cartoon'

The man behind the bar in the Ramsbottom pavilion paused in the middle of pulling my pint, fixed me with a beady if not baleful stare and advised me to take great care about what I wrote. Outsiders in general and southerners in particular tend to treat the Lancashire League in general and Ramsbottom in particular as a sort of musical hall joke. Heaven knows why, they're both remarkable and admirable institutions, but they tend to get a hostile press. The man behind the bar and Ramsbottom's genial young secretary Peter Spencer still remembered Clement Freud with disfavour. He came, saw and went away and did a hatchet job. Then one of the popular Sundays did a piece about their 1985 professional, David Hookes. Hookes, an Australian Test player, is a member of the South Australia team. The Sunday rag wanted to point the contrast between the posh Adelaide ground and poor old Rammy's pitch. They photographed Ramsbottom from all the least favourable angles and ran the predictable stuff making out that the Lancashire League Club was a down-at-heel backwater: funny name, funny place. QED.

To be absolutely honest I had something of the southerner's traditional knee-jerk reaction myself when I chose Ramsbottom as my prototype League club. I knew I would be passing by the Rossendale valley in mid-August and found the idea of a local derby between Ramsbottom and Rawtenstall irresistibly evocative. It conjured up an immediate and vivid image of a Bill Tidy cartoon with a crowd in flat caps and braces saying 'Ee bah gum.' Not that I have ever actually heard anyone in Lancashire saying 'Ee bah gum' and I don't even know what it is supposed to mean. The other games on offer were Accrington v. Nelson, Colne v. Enfield, East Lancs v. Burnley, Haslingden v. Bacup, Lowerhouse v. Rishton and Todmorden v. Church. None of those excited me in the same way as Ramsbottom v. Rawtenstall.

Jim Clarke, the League's helpful secretary, said when I asked his advice, 'I would claim in all due modesty that your question would have taxed Solomon.' He was inclined to suggest Nelson, Burnley and East Lancs on the grounds that they had won the League most often. Burnley were the top team before the Great War. After that Nelson took over, winning twice in the twenties and six times in the thirties with the help of a famous succession of professionals. The League rule is that each club has one pro at a time, and between 1920 and 1939 Nelson's were George Geary, E. A. MacDonald of Australia, J. Blankenberg of South Africa, Learie Constantine – the first coloured professional in the League's history – and Amarnath, father of Mohinder Amarnath. The great Constantine was with Nelson nine years, during

121

which they only *failed* to win the championship twice. East Lancs have won nine times since 1947. They have also had famous professionals, though some have been less successful than others. Their least triumphant import was the South African spinner, H. J. 'Toey' Tayfield, who took only 47 wickets in 1956 at an average of 15.72. Eight of them were in a single game and for only 19 runs. The East Lancs record belongs to Bruce Dooland, who took 117 wickets in 1949 at a cost of only 10.47 each.

I was tempted by all these, especially by Constantine's old club, Nelson, but they were playing away from home so I stuck with Ramsbottom. At least I intended to do that, until we stopped for lunch at a pub called the Woolpack a mile or so short of Ramsbottom. It was only when I emerged from lunch that I realised it was right opposite Haslingden's main gates. It seemed churlish to ignore the coincidence, so I wandered in.

I thought the bowler looked a bit quick, so I wasn't surprised to discover that it was Hartley Alleyne, formerly of Worcester and Barbados. Alleyne was in his third season with the club and had helped them to first and second place in the League. When I called they were lying in first place again. Alleyne is by no means the first of their imported fast bowlers. In 1981 Haslingden's pro was Andy Roberts; in 1971, Dennis Lillee.

There were about five hundred spectators in the ground. Not such a good crowd as sometimes, said the club secretary Mr Aspin, largely because the Bacup following was relatively small. For an important championship game they might get three or four thousand. For a cup-tie as many as six. Gate money last year amounted to only about three thousand pounds. It's the social side that generates profit. The bar is open all year round and turns over about £70,000 a year.

It felt prosperous and successful, with a spanking modern pavilion, large scoreboard, fixed seating and chaps on the gate taking money. I wouldn't have been at all surprised if someone had told me it was a county game on a quiet day. The standard of cricket looked quite high. 'We've produced no famous names,' said Mr Aspin, 'though our Leslie Warburton was the only man to go straight from the League to a Test trial. That was in the thirties.' They also have a young prodigy called Ian Austin, who was away playing in a junior cup competition in Cambridge but has already been busily breaking club records. Later at Ramsbottom they confirmed that young Austin was one to watch.

Whether he will eventually play for the county is another matter altogether. At both Haslingden and Ramsbottom I found them surprisingly critical of the Lancashire club and the authorities at Old Trafford. At Haslingden I was told that the young professional they engaged for 1967 would have moved on to Hampshire if it hadn't been for them. The story of Lancashire cricket would have been rather different if he *had* gone to Hampshire. His name was Clive Lloyd.

It didn't take long to drive down the valley to Ramsbottom but I missed the ground at the first attempt, and had to turn round, negotiate a roadwork inspired one-way system, and then a rather bumpy track between the river and the Trinity Paper Mill. Finally I was at Acre Bottom.

There is a move to rename the place the 'Riverside' Ground, but I hope they don't. It sounds too whimsical, and Acre Bottom is not a whimsical ground. Besides, the river is screened off from the field of play and you don't even know it's there. What I liked most about the place is the pavilion. It's the original Victorian number, newly renovated at a cost of £12,000 and painted in the club colours of green and cream. Because it is heavily timbered it has a striped effect, as if it had been papered in club ties.

Some of the immediate surroundings are a little dilapidated. Down by the river a sign says 'Snack Bar', but the snack bar was closed and likely to remain so until someone sneezes as they pass by and the thing falls down. But the setting is marvellous. Steep hills rise up on either side. From the pavilion you can look up to terraces of houses which fade away into pasture and a hill-top with that characteristic North Country juxtaposition of cows with pylon.

From the river and snack bar side the view is better still. The hill rises steeply behind the striped pavilion. At the summit there is a Peel tower. This was spoiled by scaffolding when I was there, but I gathered the scaffolding would soon be going and the Peel tower restored to its own true self. From here you can see two churches – grimy, gritty towers of St Andrew's Ramsbottom and Howcombe parish church. Those hillsides with the paper works and the old pavilion in the foreground plus the to and fro of the cricketers cry out for the brush of Lowry. Did Lowry never paint Acre Bottom? How not?

Like all good self-respecting cricket clubs they care about their past at Ramsbottom. The walls of the pavilion are a scrap-book, and like all good scrap-books they are catholic. There, above the gents is a photo of 'Owd Arthur', aka Arthur Holt who was Ramsbottom's bag carrier from 1940 to 1961. And elsewhere you can find an account of the great match between Ramsbottom and Haslingden in 1934. Five nights it lasted. Haslingden made 369 all out, of which George Headley, with 189, made more than half. Then Rammy batted and their professional, Sid Hird, made 167 not out and they won by four wickets, and the cricket correspondent of the local paper, now – man and rag – long since departed, wrote: 'It was nectar for the Gods, and we enjoyed it.'

There are distinguished old gents like Dr Crawshaw, President of the League from 1905 to 1921, and more recent characters like Seymour Nurse, who holds one of the more improbable Ramsbottom records. On 8 July 1961 Ramsbottom, replying to Enfield's 156, were 57 for three. Nurse, the third man out, had scored all 57.

Gordon Horrocks & Les Bamor.

In the very old days at the end of the nineteenth century Ramsbottom, like their rivals, always had a brace of pros: Whittaker and Jackson; Town and Hatfield; Shacklock and White. Since 1900 they have just had the one, but there are some great names among them. Peter Spencer told me that at one moment during the 1985 Test series against the Australians the men in the Channel Nine commentary box were Ian Chappell, Keith Stackpole and David Hookes. Each one of them is a former Ramsbottom professional. And when they came to evaluate the performance of Murray Bennett in his curious dark glasses they were not just passing judgement on another Australian Test cricketer but on yet another Ramsbottom professional.

Not that all the good Ramsbottom players have made their mark elsewhere; and certainly not where you would most expect it. Just as at Haslingden I heard a consistent bad-mouthing of Old Trafford and the Lancashire club. 'Year in year out,' I was told, 'Lancashire League clubs have a couple of amateurs who could make the grade at first-class level. But time and again they're ignored. You'll find some newcomer playing for the county and ask where he's from and they'll tell you from the Cheshire League or something.'

That evening Peter Spencer had organised a special brains trust. Notts were playing Lancashire and four of them - Rice, Hadlee, Randall and either Broad or Robinson - were driving out after stumps for a mixture of fun and fund-raising. Rice was the Ramsbottom man. The South African captain of Nottingham, holder of the Silk Cut Trophy for the best all-rounder in the world, was the club professional in 1973 and helped them to the Holland Cup, awarded to the League runners-up. Ramsbottom were impressed by Rice and sent him over to Old Trafford for a trial. Old Trafford sent him back, with words to the effect that 'he'll never make a cricketer'. So he went to Trent Bridge instead.

There are exceptions. Of the present Lancashire team Jack Simmons used to be an amateur with the Lancashire League team, Enfield. And Enfield produced probably the most famous of all League emeriti, Eddie Paynter, who was presented with a pair of silver candlesticks by the League for his stirring deeds for England against Australia.

But just as often the League men go to other counties. The one and only Tony Lock, for instance, was the Ramsbottom pro in 1965, then went off to Leicester as captain, where he was still a good enough bowler to take 272 wickets at eighteen apiece. Kevin Curran played for Rawtenstall before going to Gloucester. Bill Alley was the pro at Colne and the first man in League history ever to score a thousand runs in five successive seasons. That was five years before he embarked on that wonderful Indian summer down in Somerset. In 1939 five Bacup men were playing first-class cricket – only two for Lancashire. In 1949 five Todmorden players were with counties: Shackleton and Dawson with Hampshire, Horsfall with Essex, Fiddling with Northants and only Greenwood with Lancashire. Worth recalling that although Greenwood took more than two hundred wickets for Lancashire, Shackleton took more than two thousand for Hampshire.

The Lancashire League has four 'Objects', baldly stated as such at the beginning of the annual report:

'To promote a greater interest in the game.

'To foster and develop local Amateur talent.

'To inspire punctuality in the matches, and to arrange an annual competition among its members.

'To control Professionalism.'

To this end the rules stipulate one pro and ten amateurs. And each amateur must be born in the town or have lived there for twelve months or have been in business there for twelve months. It's not like the other side of the Pennines where, if they happen not to have a county match, you'll find half the Yorkshire team playing for some League side. It couldn't happen in the Lancashire League, where there are the fiercest rules about amateurs. The only times an amateur makes money are when he hits fifty or takes five for under 40, six for under 48, seven for under 56, or eight or more for anything. When that happens they pass round the hat.

I was much impressed by what I saw of the League and especially by Ramsbottom Cricket Club and their green and cream ground at Acre Bottom. The cricket is reason enough, but there is more to it than that. A notice at Ramsbottom CC says, quite properly, 'Pleasant Pavilion Bar – Open Seven Days Each Week.' Would that they could boast as much in St John's Wood.

NEW ROAD, WORCESTER

*'I would still not be
surprised to see a
57-year-old
clergyman
coming on to bowl'*

One of the great visual clichés of cricket is Worcester Cathedral. As a backcloth it is rivalled only by the Lord's pavilion and the Oval gasholders, and it is older and more beautiful than either; older and more beautiful than any other cricketing landmark in the country. On 7 June 1218, long before cricket was played in the county, there was a great service to celebrate the restoration of the cathedral after the fires of 1189 and 1202.

King Henry III, then a boy of ten, attended along with eleven bishops, seventeen abbots, assorted priors and the greatest nobles in the land. That day the church was formally dedicated to St Mary and St Peter and the blessed Confessors, St Oswald and St Wulstan. The last two are Worcester's very own saints – local lads made very good indeed.

However keen you are on cricket, I think you should drop in on the Cathedral first. Observe the plaque commemorating the two Perownes, father and son, both bishops of Worcester; and the memorials to Edward Elgar, and Stanley Baldwin, and Sir John and Lady Beauchamp, their heads resting on two exquisite black swans; and bad King John, with his feet on the body of a dog with its tail between its legs. Consider the Rev. Geoffrey Kennedy MC, known as 'Woodbine Willie' from his habit of doling out cigarettes to the Tommies in the First World War. And reflect on poor Prince Arthur, Henry VIII's elder brother and first husband of Catharine of Aragon. Think of Housman and 'In Summertime on Bredon/The bells they sound so clear' and pause, as you will have to, by the verbose memorial to 'The most excellent prelate, Dr John Hough, the ever memorable president of Magdalen College, Oxford.'

You have to pause here because you can only climb to the top of the tower with an escort, and the escort only goes up at prescribed times. It's a long climb and gets narrow near the top, but it is worth it. From the summit you can gaze down across the Severn and reverse the cliché by looking down on the cricket from the great church tower. Never mind that when I was there the rain came scudding across the city and little matchstick men could be seen pushing covers out on to the tiny wicket. Never mind that it was grey. This is how you should catch your first sight of the County Ground at Worcester.

In 1896 those green acres were farmland belonging to the Dean and Chapter. There were three fields with a hedge through the middle, and a hayrick. Paul Foley, the first secretary of the county club, rented the fields from the Dean, and hired an inspired groundsman, from Berkshire, called Fred Hunt. In 1899 Worcester were admitted to the County Championship; spectator seating had been installed and so had a telegraph for the press. On the morning of 4 May Mr Foley, in his usual brown bowler and boots, was personally applying a final coat of paint to the sightscreen. At noon Tunnicliffe and Brown, the Yorkshire openers, came out to bat. After three balls Brown went back again, his middle stump knocked out by Worcester's G. A. Wilson. Wilson bowled fast round-arm off a surprisingly short run.

The *Worcester Journal* described it as 'A Grand Beginning in First Class' and went on: 'There was bright genial sunshine for the opening of this cricket match on the New Road ground. Everything was of the happiest augury for the debut of Worcestershire in first-class cricket. Mr Foley, Mr Isaac and others had been at work from soon after dawn to put the finishing touches to the arrangements. Everything looked as pleasant as one could desire.'

The bright genial sunshine was late in coming the day I was there, and the umpires, Bird and Palmer, abandoned play for the day just as I walked into the ground. 'A bit premature in my estimation,' said one member stomping into the old pavilion and ordering a 'scotch and dry, darling'. The rumour was that one or two of the players wanted to go fishing. The next day they were staging a big match – the NatWest semi-final against Nottingham – and my own suspicion was that the Worcester secretary, Mike Vockins, was quite happy to be able to get on with preparing for that. There were crush barriers to go up and portable red bucket seats and television gantries and more sponsors' signs and hoardings than seemed quite decent. There were ladders going up on the front of the scoreboard, causing an anxious Vockins to call across and ask what was going on. Then he had to refer to the rules to see whether advertising was allowed there or not. A county secretary has much to contend with. While I was talking to him he was the only person in the office. The phone went.

'I've no idea,' he said, quite politely but with a hint of exasperation, then listened for a few moments.

'I'm sorry,' he said eventually. 'All I can advise is that you check the weather forecast on TV.'

He put the phone down and grinned. 'Man from Nottingham,' he explained, 'who wanted me to tell him categorically whether or not there would be any play tomorrow and was it worth his coming.' He sighed.

Outside, although there was no play, there was still an air of bustle and anticipation. There are some new buildings and improvements have been carried out to dressing-rooms. Inevitably there is a new 'Executive Suite' but generally speaking the atmosphere remains rustic and traditional. 'We're in a conservation area anyway,' says Vockins, 'and we are more or less committed to the idea that Worcester is wonderful as it is.'

Certainly the view from the pavilion is every bit as good as the pictures suggest. It is wider than I had thought, with the cathedral slightly less dominant and a fine spire to the left which is all that remains of St Andrew's Church and is known locally as 'The Glover's

Needle'. There used to be glovemaking factories all along the banks of the Severn.

One critic has remarked that Worcester is in danger of 'prettying too much its ground'. He was unhappy about the 'sponsored flowers'. There are a considerable number of tubs and hanging baskets 'supplied by Webbs Garden centres of Wychbold, Droitwich, Weobley and Stourbridge', and I am entirely in favour of them. They have also been busy planting trees, including a black pear tree to one side of the Ladies' Pavilion, where there are still comfortable chintz-covered chairs reserved for the exclusive use of Lady Members. The black pear tree is highly significant but turned out to be rather disappointing. Planted to celebrate the club centenary in 1965, it is a fairly weedy tree, nothing like as big and virile as my own comice, and the pears themselves were scrawny and not black at all, just mottled green like any other pear.

The story is that when Elizabeth I visited Worcester in 1575 she was given some black pears whereupon she said the city could use three of them in their coat of arms. The County Cricket Club crest, adapted from the county crest in 1899, is 'a shield argent bearing a fess between three pears sable'. The centre lines running across the middle of the shield are wavy, dark blue at the edges and light in the centre. They represent – of course – the River Severn.

You can't see the river from the ground, but it plays an important role in the ground's life, flooding the field frequently in winter and giving rise to a considerable folklore. The original groundsman, Fred

Hunt, is reputed to have caught a 45-pound salmon on the ground, and it is also alleged that one year a large salmon was left stranded when a flood subsided. High tide marks are recorded and the annual report has a picture of the present groundsman and colleague manoeuvring a rowing boat across the placid waters of the square. It doesn't seem to harm the playing surface.

In the absence of the players who should have been performing the most visible star was Basil d'Oliveira, a graceful and brilliant all-rounder in his playing days, and now the club coach as well as father of one of the current generation of Worcestershire players. Dolly was wandering about the place in a green track-suit. He looked thoughtful, and portlier than I remembered. Nevertheless he is one of those authentically famous cricketers who get pointed at and nudged about. He was thirty-three when he first came to England, yet he played in forty-four Tests. For me, he and Tom Graveney epitomised Worcestershire in the sixties when they won the championship twice in successive years after ninety-eight with nothing. Both had the priceless quality of making the game look easy, and fun too.

Worcester is the smallest of all the first-class counties, and it has gone through some uncomfortable periods. In its early years the club was constantly in debt and always being underwritten by the secretary. The present president is the Duke of Westminster, who plays a little, and has staged benefit matches at Eaton Hall, his home in Cheshire. Since he is reputed to be the richest man in England the financial future shouldn't be too dim.

In cricketing terms the past has been chequered. In those earliest years they were dominated by the Foster family. The Reverend Foster was a housemaster at Malvern. All seven of his Malvernian sons played for the county, and three – H.K., R.E. and M.K. – captained them for almost twenty years between them. They called the county Fostershire. There are few echoes of Fostershire around the New Road ground now but there are some photographs and mementoes. Major Jewell's 1929 team, for instance. And Captain W.H. Shakespeare, MC, AFC, pictured in 1919, dashing with cravat and moustache; and the same man more than fifty years on when he was president in 1974 and the county won their third championship and he still had a moustache and an OBE as well. In the old pavilion there is a picture of W.G with the caption 'It's your round'; and there is Fred Bowley's bat. Bowley hit 276 with it against Hampshire in 1914. And there is a bat of Don Kenyon's too. It's badly split.

I met a man at the river end who was a Kenyon worshipper. 'I don't think we'll ever have another Glenn Turner,' he said wistfully. 'He was the best to watch, if you know what I mean, like. But the Don. The Don was actually my favourite, if you know what I mean.' He had seen Colin Milburn get a pair one year and he remembered the crowds queueing for the Australian match in 1948. They stretched right back over the Severn Bridge and 14,000 got into the ground. That was the biggest crowd they've ever had at Worcester and Bradman failed. He only made 107. He had been three times before and on each occasion he had made a double century.

I think that the Worcester player I would most like to have seen is George Simpson-Hayward. Like the Fosters he was a Malvernian and he bowled right-arm lobs which spun wickedly. He got six for 45 against South Africa in his first Test and he took 362 wickets for Worcester at an average of 22.68. He was the last of the great under-arm bowlers. He was also the first captain of the county to take the club to the bottom of the championship, a prelude to some very bad years indeed. After the first war they did not even resume first-class cricket at once. When they did in 1920, *Wisden* remarked, 'Sorry as one may feel for Worcestershire, there is no getting away from the fact that their return to the Championship was a complete failure.' Some very unlikely people played for Worcester in those years. They used thirty-seven different players in 1922. One of them was the Reverend R. H. Moss who played once in 1925 aged fifty-seven. He scored two runs and took one for five.

Of all the county headquarters Worcester is the most bucolic and seems likely to remain so. Historically I find the combination of such very prosaic professional names and such wonderfully languid aristo-cratic ones quite irresistible. Oh to have seen Root's nine for 23 on this ground against Lancashire in 1931; or the Nawab of Pataudi's 231 not out against Essex two years later; or his 224 not out against Kent the same year. He made 214 not out against Glamorgan a year after that. Their captains have been Fosters and Ponsonby and Major Jew-ell, and the Hon. J. B. Coventry and the Hon. Charles Lyttelton, and their most successful bowlers Perks and Root.

One of the oddest pictures in the Worcester collection is a photo-graph of the 1895 match between the Gentlemen of Worcestershire and All Holland. I found it very difficult to work out which are the Gentlemen and which the Dutchmen. Van den Berg and Oldenboom, Kuffa and Posthuma, Powys-Keck and Burnup. No such games are played at Worcester any longer, and it has to be said that the present Worcester team, promising and young though it is, lacks something of the diversity and panache I associate with Worcester history.

The ground, however, has retained its character. Of all the county grounds of England Worcester strikes me as the one which remains most redolent of the curious cricketing past. I suppose the cathedral helps, but I would still not be altogether surprised to see a 57-year-old clergyman coming on to bowl at Worcester. Nor a bevy of Foster brothers batting, or a man with a fine moustache and a double-bar-relled name bowling under-arm spin. Ninety years on it is still, I feel, one of the few grounds fit to stage a match between All Holland and the Gentlemen of the County.

HEADINGLEY

'Must do summat
about beer
in Winter Shed'

I have nothing against Yorkshire, much less Yorkshire cricket. Most sporting allegiances are formed young, and as a child in the 1950s I tended to be a Yorkshire supporter. There was little logic in this. My preparatory school was in Somerset but though I was fond of Somerset it was plainly an act of masochism to identify too closely with such a band of hopelessness. We lived near Gerrards Cross, from which the trains ran into Marylebone itself, so Lord's was the home ground and Denis Compton the local hero. I ought to have supported Middlesex – or, failing that, Surrey, who won the championship every summer of my prep school life. Little boys love a winner and I could quite easily have chosen Surrey. But no, it was Yorkshire I backed, and Yorkshire whose scores I turned to first in the morning paper or listened for most avidly on the Home Service.

I think it must have been something to do with Hutton. Or Johnny Wardle. Or Trueman. Or Willie Watson. They were a tremendous team on paper, but they didn't win a championship until near the end of the fifties when Hutton, Appleyard, Watson and Wardle had all gone. I never really understood what all the fuss over Wardle was about, but I do remember being depressed, although my support never wavered. Latterly there had been a reconciliation between Wardle and his old county and he was retained as an adviser on bowling. He had also emerged as an expert on pitches and wickets and I had hoped to talk to him for this book. Sadly he suffered a brain haemorrhage in 1985 and died that summer.

I continued supporting Yorkshire over the years, a perverse affiliation whose conviction diminished almost annually. Like Newcastle United, whom I supported for similar reasons, Yorkshire County Cricket Club seems always to be its own worst enemy. The Wardle affair was bad enough but time and again the best Yorkshiremen left for other pastures where, inevitably, they seemed to perform with a zestful success which made their old county look ridiculous. Close to Somerset and Illingworth to Leicester are the most obvious examples. Most recently it has been Athey to Gloucester.

Everyone now knows that there is some sort of running crisis in Yorkshire cricket and that it presently centres on the person of Geoffrey Boycott. The precise nature of this controversy is as elusive as the precise nature of the Schleswig-Holstein affair – and about as interesting for the non-aligned. All one can say for certain is that it has a debilitating effect on the cricket. The 1984 annual report recorded, without comment: 'Special General Meeting. This took place at the Conference Centre, Harrogate, on the 21st January 1984, when resolutions were carried of No Confidence in both the Cricket sub-committee and the General Committee, and urging a further one-year playing contract to be offered to Geoffrey Boycott. This in turn involved the resignation of the Committee, and at the resulting district elections there were many new members elected.' That sort of Special General Meeting is routine stuff these days.

I had been to Old Trafford for the first half of the Roses' duel, so it seemed appropriate to visit Headingley for the second. Contrary to my normal practice I drove to Headingley, combining business with a family holiday in the Yorkshire Dales. That night we stayed in a pub in north Notts which had the world's second most uncomfortable bed, a regular supply of heavy lorries passing within inches of the bedroom window and a late closing juke box immediately below. That, coupled with a long bewildered loop round the Leeds ring road before a crawl through the town centre, put me in a less enthusiastic mood than I would have liked.

You should take the Otley road (pronounced Otla with a sharp accent on the last syllable), continue until the Headingley War Memorial which is between two pubs, one of which sells Tetley's, the other Whitbread 'Yorkshire Brewed Ales'.

I parked in Ash Gardens, walked down Derwentwater Grove and into Headingley View. Later on I saw some villas with names, but here I was struck by the lack of pretension. A true Yorkshire characteristic, I suppose, a reflection of the Yorkshireman's devotion to plain speaking and calling spades bloody shovels. These houses, numbered not named, and almost painfully plain, were making a statement all right. The statement was 'A house is a house is a house'. Opposite the Headingley turnstiles there were two shops. Mr Saffer, the pharmacist, had no protection on his glass window; Mr Luharia had metal mesh grills all over his general stores. I judged this not just to be because he had a licence to sell wines and spirits, whereas the pharmacist traded in little more exciting than sponges, but because he appeared to be of Asian origin. Maybe I was being cynical.

There was some dispute next day over the size of the crowd. The *Observer* said 5,000, the *Sunday Times* 4,000 and the *Sunday Telegraph* 'fewer than 2,000'. I have always been dubious about crowd estimates. All I can say is that there was an agreeable if not exactly hectic sense of bustle and anticipation about the place. People were heading towards the ground with quick tread and lunch bag, looking eager. As we calculated our admission at the turnstiles a friendly middle-aged man with a haversack strapped to his back swept my elder son off through the members' entrance with a cheery 'I'll take the lad in', which saved us a few bob. Like most county matches (though not always cup-ties) this one was reasonably priced, but six admissions are never cheap. The member's gesture was appreciated.

While on the subject of finance, I couldn't help noticing that Yorkshire charge 25p for their scorecards. For the corresponding fixture at

Old Trafford I was charged 10p. Notts and Worcester charge ten, too; Leicester fifteen. It is true that the Yorkshire card is better printed than most and on better card; but it is – like others – subsidised by advertisements from the likes of Yorkshire Microcomputers, Austin Steel of Dewsbury, and Cleanaway Waste Services of Ravensthorpe. A small point, I suppose, but I did feel I wasn't getting value for money.

I had hoped to see Boycott on his home turf, but it was not to be. The Master had tweaked a hamstring – or something like that. Old age seems to have made him very cautious, but I retain a sneaking admiration for him if only because I was at Lord's that magical day when he made his great century in the final of the Gillette Cup. No one who was there can ever think of him as boring, but then I know people who used to say the same of poor Ken Barrington and I never believed them.

I was sorry not to see him ambling about on the boundary, chewing gun with that introspective, quizzical grin. He hit three sixes and fifteen fours on that magical September day at Lord's in 1965. He and Brian Close carted Surrey all over the ground. Illingworth and Trueman did the bowling damage. Illingworth had five and Fred got Edrich, Smith and Barrington in a single over. That was the last Yorkshire team I think I came close to worshipping.

Not only, I read in the morning's paper, was Boycott missing but

Sidebottom too. And Lancashire were without Graham Fowler, Clive Lloyd (attending Forbes Burnham's funeral in Guyana) and Jack Simmons. Indeed Lancashire had only four capped players in the team and Yorkshire's star bowler, Shaw, was a twenty-two-year-old electrician from the Coal Board.

Lancashire were batting, the sophisticated electronic scoreboard told us. No wickets down. To someone who had only ever seen Headingley on television the place was a considerable shock. On TV you see little other than close-ups of the play which include only occasional glimpses of the advertising boards and a blur of the front row spectators in the background. Apart from the scoreboard, all you see of the ground is the odd shot of the pavilion when people leave and enter the playing arena.

The Headingley pavilion is a remarkably dull do.

Technically it is only half a pavilion. It is not a place for Yorkshire members but houses the players and Joe Lister, the county secretary, who inhabits the ground floor. Mr Lister played for the county briefly in 1954, the year he joined Worcester as assistant secretary. He scored thirty-five runs for Yorkshire, averaging just under nine. Yet another example of a modest player turning his hand to some other aspect of the game and becoming a power in the cricketing land. He has been secretary at Yorkshire since 1971. His office is perfectly all right, but the building is dull and small. On television, however, it is practically all one sees, which had led me to suppose that the Headingley ground was newish, smallish and undistinguished.

Not so at all. In real life Headingley, which claims a capacity of 20,000, feels enormous and far more ancient than modern. Entering by the turnstile near the 'Winter Shed', I was immediately aware of a great bank of uncovered wooden seating to my right, a huge football stand presenting its backside to me and what appeared to be a beached aircraft carrier. The wicket seems miles away, partly because an ancient cycle track rings the perimeter between most of the seats and the field of play.

Norman Yardley, who was after all captain of Yorkshire from 1948 to 1955 and might be expected to feel some loyalty to the place, wrote that 'the amenities for spectators cannot be ranked very high. Refreshment arrangements are decidedly utilitarian.' Now as then the main ordinary spectators' bar and refreshment area is in the 'Winter Shed'. This is no misnomer. In winter it serves as the indoor cricket school. In summer it is a cavernous canteen serving bitter and singularly unimaginative old-fashioned pies and butties. One thing struck me as very odd. Although Yorkshire has rightly famous beers from such breweries as Theakston's, John Smith and Goose Eye, at the ground they seemed only to be selling Younger's 'Scotch bitter'.

The ground looks better if you move round to the rugby stand end and go to the top of the terracing. From there the backdrop is a line of poplars, planted, it is sometimes alleged, to block the view from the gardens of the houses beyond. A number of trees were looking rather dead and one spectator even suggested the householders might have been sabotaging them with weedkiller. Behind them on the hill is St Mary's Church with a tall, if grimey, spire. Below it, invisible even from the high terracing, is the Oak Fisheries, where to judge from the lunchtime queue a number of spectators reckon you can get a better meal than in the Winter Shed.

Although there is no mistaking that the big grandstand was designed for the benefit of those watching the rugby on the other side, there are seats facing the cricket and even some concessions to the glorious cricketing past. There is a Len Hutton bar. In the 'aircraft carrier', which turns out to be the old pavilion in disguise, there are photographs, though once again rugby league seems to get more space than cricket. And the cricket is not all Yorkshire by any means. I was surprised to find one of the match played at Lord's between the smokers and the non-smokers of England and Australia in 1884. It feels more like a snug winter hideout than an airy cricket-watching place. Anyone seeing Headingley for the first time and being told that this was the headquarters of the most famous and successful of all the English cricketing counties could be forgiven for being somewhat sceptical.

The reason for this was explained, at least in part, by Joe Lister. It transpires that Yorkshire, in one vital respect, are way back where Leicester and Essex were after the last war. They are homeless vagabonds. 'Yorkshire,' he told me, 'does not own a blade of grass or a plank of wood.' They play throughout the old county, paying no attention to 'reforms' which have placed part of Yorkshire in Humberside. 'Headingley,' he says, 'is owned by the Leeds Cricket, Football and Athletic Company. And effectively that means the rugby league club.' What *that* means, effectively, is that Yorkshire are not truly masters in their own house.

Not that there haven't been improvements. The sophisticated electronic scoreboard, which was probably before its time and was initially accident-prone, has now been reprogrammed by Professor Jim Briggs of Sheffield University and seems to have overcome its teething troubles. There are executive boxes above the Winter Shed and a 'White Rose Executive Club'.

But the over-riding impression is one of conservatism. The club stands alone in refusing to play other than Yorkshire-born players. They still produce an annual hardbound yearbook in the same way they always have - other counties have changed to paperback. And despite the squabbling they are well served by officials who sometimes seem to go on for ever. In over a hundred and twenty years they have had only nine presidents, eight treasurers and five secretaries.

Great deeds have been done at Headingley, most notably in that extraordinary 1981 match between England and Australia when Botham made one of his extraordinary centuries. Somerset once scored 630 here; Verity took ten for 32 against Warwickshire; the Australians were bowled out by Yorkshire for 23 in 1902; though in 1933 the county made only 33 all out against Lancashire. Sutcliffe and Leyland both made two double-centuries on this ground.

Nothing like that happened when I was there. One observer of the '85 Yorkshire team remarked that they looked like a school first XI. That day against Lancashire they were missing all three of their capped seam bowlers and only Bairstow, the skipper behind the stumps, exuded maturity. There seemed to be a lot of chat coming from the field of play and I assume most of it was coming from Bairstow. He is a good player to watch – combative and chirpy – but I felt he needed a few more supportive old pros to help him along.

The Coal Board electrician looked sharp enough. But Lancashire took the honours and young Fairbrother made his second Roses century of the summer. The sun shone too. I just wish that Yorkshire could start to win things again and that a Yorkshireman or two could win a regular England place. No England team seems complete without one. And they must do summat about beer in Winter Shed.

THE RACECOURSE
GROUND, DERBY

*'The finest straight
mile in England'*

I was prejudiced in favour of the county ground at Derby long before I saw it. Everywhere on the county circuit men shook their heads and grumbled when you mentioned Derby. It was ugly. It was uncomfortable. Nothing had been spent on it for years. It was a disgrace to the game. Several people told me that the Derby and England fast bowler, Mike Hendrick, had left the club because of the shocking state of the players' lavatories. Now Chesterfield, ah, yes, Chesterfield, that was a cricket ground. One of the most beautiful grounds in England. Dozens of old cricketing bores waxed lyrical about the crooked spire of the Chesterfield church to such an extent that I became perverse. I was not going to even look at Chesterfield, but I was going to Derby and I was determined to like it.

I thought my instincts were right when I paused at the entrance and one of the gatemen, an elderly man of the kind you learn to recognise once you have passed through more than a dozen county ground turnstiles, gazed through the drizzle at the dank green turf and the dilapidated old grandstand and said, 'That used to be the finest straight mile in England.'

When, at the office, I asked if anyone knew where I would find the secretary, Roger Pearman, I was told that the 'chief executive' would probably be upstairs in the pavilion. Elsewhere on the circuit Mr Pearman would be called the secretary or, just conceivably, the secretary-manager. Since Derby is probably the least fashionable and grand of all the seventeen first-class counties, it is entirely predictable that they call Mr Pearman their 'chief executive'. They are compensating.

Fearful rows erupted under Mr Pearman in the autumn of 1983. They led to a Special General Meeting chaired by no less a personage than the President of the Club, His Grace the Duke of Devonshire. The Annual Report had a wonderfully succinct account of the proceedings. That September some committee members walked out of a meeting after a Mr Osborne made a 'concerted attack' on the chief executive. When His Grace invited questions and comments from the floor, Mr Osborne said they did not want Mr Pearman to continue as chief executive. A chief executive, it seemed, should behave like one and stay behind his desk in his office. Mr Pearman was much too inclined to mingle with the players and the punters, exchanging pleasantries and buying his round.

It all sounds quite as ugly and divided as anything that goes on north of the border in the land of the White Rose. However, when I arrived it was plain that Mr Pearman was still in charge, and very much at ease both with his committee and with the players.

It was not, however, his continued tenure of office, nor the fact that he was in the top of the pavilion which pleased me. When I introduced myself he was with a rather grizzled, smallish chap who had that unmistakable combination of tweed, authority and reduced but middle-class circumstance which defines the schoolmaster. This turned out to be the former headmaster of Pocklington School, York, one Guy Willatt, ex-captain of the county and now a leading committee member. Mr Willatt immediately endeared himself to me by saying that he had recently read a novel of mine. What's more he had enjoyed it. There is nothing a writer likes more than that rare bird, the appreciative reader. So at this point I became firmly convinced that I was going to like Derby.

I am not sure whether I could find the ground again. Maybe it was because I got there early and did not take the direct route. Derby is a railway town, of course. I passed that Great White Elephant, the Advanced Passenger Train, as my own train drew into the station, which is itself in the process of being refurbished. Outside the entrance there is a hugely grand war memorial to 'the brave men of the Midland Railway' who gave their lives.... Everywhere around the station are dull red-brick railway cottages and buildings and decaying workshops. For anyone who regrets the passing of the railway era Derby is a sad place of pilgrimage.

The cathedral was naturally the reason for not proceeding directly to the ground. It is not one of the great cathedrals, in fact it is not really a cathedral at all, but the Parish Church of All Saints, designated a cathedral in the C. of E.'s 1927 boundary reform, which created the diocese of Derby from parts of Lichfield to the west and Southwell to the east. The fine medieval tower is, however, clearly visible from the ground; and the president of the club's most redoubtable ancestress, Bess of Hardwick, is entombed within. The church itself is mainly eighteenth-century because one of the vicars, Dr Hutchinson, had the medieval one knocked down and engaged the architect James Gibbs to build a new church. The official guide says, 'The classical design makes no concessions to the exuberant gothic of the tower, but they live harmoniously together.' This is the sort of remark I should like to hear said aloud by a guide from the Aesthetic Tendency.

By the time I had cased the cathedral the early promise had turned to wet, so I hurried into a tea shop above a pub where the proprietor was saying to the other two customers: 'Good morning ladies, horrible morning!' I lingered over a pot of tea and a toasted tea-cake (50p), but even so the drizzle was still descending. Mr Pearman told me later that Derby was a football town, even when County were in the third division, so it wasn't surprising that people's directions to the cricket were confused. It turned out to be on the wrong side of a dual carriageway swirling with traffic. Not a long walk, but not a nice one either.

I would have known at once that it was an old racecourse even if the gateman had not told me it was the best straight mile in England. The old stand topped with a venerable verdegris cupola is still there. So is the starter's box, and the jockeys' changing-rooms. But, contrary to popular opinion elsewhere, there is now a modern pavilion with long room, bar, executive suites and a balcony. It is not, to my eye, the world's most beautiful building, and like almost all modern cricket pavilions it lacks the style of the Victorians and Edwardians. It cries out for some wrought iron work, for a mad clock tower or a batty belfry. But still it is there with all mod cons and a plaque which says, 'The Foundation Stone was laid on the 23rd January 1982 by the Mayor of Derby, Councillor Flo Tunnicliffe.'

Elsewhere it must be admitted there is still some dilapidation and decay, and at least one area is cordoned off with a sign saying, 'This stand must not be used today.' But Derby's long overdue facelift does seem to have begun.

Some of Derby's problems may stem from it not being a cricket town, but that in itself is a chicken and egg situation. It's not just that the facilities have been so poor – the cricket has often seemed pawky and they have won fewer pots than most. Their most recent success was the NatWest trophy in 1981, and they did manage a championship in 1936. The photograph of the winning team hangs in the new pavilion and was explained to me by a steward who remembered watching them.

I quickly saw what Mr Pearman meant about Derby being a football town: 'Jack Bennett,' said my friend. 'He was the trainer with Coventry City. Harry Storer – he played for Derby County and was Manager of Derby County and Coventry City.' Their footballing prowess was as important as their cricketing skill. The captain was A. W. Richardson, 'owner of a family business in Derby'. Then there was Alf Pope, and Harry Elliott and Bill Copson and Tommy Mitchell. My informant punctuated his rather lugubrious litany with: 'He's passed on' or 'He's still knocking around.' I have to confess the names meant very little to me and when I checked to see what Christopher Martin-Jenkins said of them in the *Wisden Book of Cricket*, I was not surprised to find such phrases as 'hard-headed, efficient cricketers' and that back-handed catch-all, 'considerable character'.

Not that Derby doesn't excite enthusiasm and even passion. A few months before visiting the ground I had been at Eyam, the famous Derbyshire plague village which had gone into voluntary isolation when the disease spread there in the seventeenth century from London. There in the churchyard was the grave of Harry Bagshaw, a Derby all-rounder from 1887 to 1902. He subsequently became an umpire. The tombstone shows an umpire's hand signalling 'Out' as Bagshaw's wicket goes down for the very last time. What I had not realised until reading it in the county yearbook was that Bagshaw was buried in an

Ken Roe.

umpire's coat with six pebbles in one pocket. He was holding a cricket ball in one hand.

They have had some famous players, too, including exiles from the north like Barry Wood and John Hampshire, and from further afield. Eddie Barlow, the South African, captained them from 1976–78. While I was there the best-known Derby player was the lissom Michael Holding, pitted this time against his fellow West Indian exile, Joel Garner of Somerset. (Play started late, after lunch, and Derby were quickly in trouble against the 'Big Bird' in the damp.) Perhaps Derby's most famous captain was the Australian 'Demon', F. R. Spofforth, who married a girl from Birdsall. Unfortunately Spofforth captained them in 1890, after they had been deprived of first-class status for losing too many games. It was Spofforth who discovered that the assistant secretary, Samuel Richardson, had absconded with most of the club's cash. Richardson, a former captain of the club, fled to Spain, where he changed his name and became official tailor to the Court of King Alfonso.

They have home-grown stars, too. Geoff Miller, their England all-rounder, was born in Chesterfield, and Bob Taylor, who holds the world record for dismissals by a wicket-keeper, is from Staffordshire,

which is the next best thing. He had 1,471 catches and 175 stumpings. Over the years there has been a profitable association with the local public school, Repton, although the abolition of the amateur–professional distinction in 1963 has diminished its importance. Nine Repton blues played for the county and the side has also included Repton schoolmasters like J. D. Eggar. Two Reptonians have captained Derbyshire - D. B. Carr, now secretary of the Test and County Cricket Cricket Board, and G. L. Willatt. I was reminded of this on encountering Mr Willatt, my reader, as we both walked the perimeter of the racecourse ground.

He was standing by the sightscreen, and as we looked out at the modest gables of the new pavilion and the little spring onion cupola on the grandstand, he told me how he came to Derby. At Cambridge, where he was captain, he played vacation cricket for Notts; then he became a schoolmaster and played no first-class cricket for a while until Derbyshire and Repton cobbled together a remarkable deal. The convention in those days - the fifties - was still that counties were captained by an amateur. Derby invited Willatt to take the job. Repton were anxious to engage him as a schoolmaster and also made an approach. Repton, however, were not keen to take him on for only two terms a year while he played cricket all summer, and certainly weren't prepared to pay him in absentia. Derby couldn't pay him, because if they did he would have lost his amateur status. So it was agreed that Repton paid him for the autumn and spring terms; then he left to play cricket. Repton continued to pay him but were reimbursed by the county cricket club, who paid the school to hire a temporary replacement. Thus was the myth of the amateur skipper preserved!

Times were changing even then. 'There was an old wooden pavilion then,' he told me (wicket and ground were then in a different position, even further away from the old grandstand), 'and there was one big dressing-room for the amateurs and one much smaller one for the pros, of whom, of course, there were many more. I insisted on the same dressing-room for everyone. My chairman was horrified.'

It must have been a grim, windswept place. The players sat in the starter's box; there wasn't even a white boundary fence until 1980. There is now a mound and trees to give some shelter, but it used to be one of the bleakest grounds in the country as well as one of the biggest. In fact, although it may not actually be, it *feels* like the biggest county ground in England.

It is never going to be cosy, whatever they do with it, but I like the atmosphere. I liked the banter among the old sweats with the public address system up in the starter's box. Mr Pearman, over a beer in the pavilion, said in the prescribed chief executive's manner, 'We're still lacking facilities for the ordinary punter.' I suppose he's right, but they have cricket and you can see the medieval tower of the quasi-cathedral; and the Grandstand Hotel, the pub under the stand, at the far end away from the new pavilion, does good food and a decent pint, and the ordinary punters in there, waiting for Joel Garner to have a go at the young Derby batsmen, seemed to be happy enough. One ordinary punter who had kept his hat on and was wearing his tie outside the pullover under his jacket was holding forth to all and sundry the way ordinary punters do. ''E *is* a good bat,' he said, splashing the beer from his straight-sided glass as he waved it about. ''E *is* a good bat. I've seen 'im opening for Second XI. But it's bloody bowlers we want, not bloody batsmen.'

And when he had finished another ordinary punter regarded him thoughtfully and said, ''Ave yer done?'

That day's *Derby Evening Telegraph* had a headline over the cricket report which said, 'No Miracle for Derbyshire this time round', and I wouldn't expect many real miracles this time round, nor for a few rounds yet. At the same time I'd as soon be in Derby on a summer cricket day, however grey, than in a few more widely touted spots. But perhaps that is just because it was the only county ground in England where I met a committee member who had read one of my books.

CANTERBURY

'August Bank Holiday – no business lunch'

The 1985 Australian tourists were not one of the great cricket teams, but there were times when they looked the part. At Canterbury on a pleasant shirt-sleeve order day Border and Ritchie whacked some very ordinary Kent bowling to all corners of the field. One lofted drive of Ritchie's smashed straight through the windscreen of a yellow Volkswagen which had parked culpably close to the long-on boundary. Serve the owner right, I thought. Present a glass front to a batsman like that, especially when he is facing bowlers like them, and you are asking for trouble.

I felt a certain more general satisfaction over the incident because Canterbury is one of those grounds that everyone enthuses about, like Arundel or Worcester. And yet aesthetically it is spoiled if not ruined by allowing cars to park around much of the perimeter just over the boundary fence. Yes, yes, there is a funny old pavilion and the eccentric tree on the field of play and the famous memorials to Blythe and Fuller Pilch, and yet, on a busy day like the one I was there, it's a little like watching a game of cricket in the middle of the Motor Show.

It does something else, too. At grounds like Chelmsford, say, or Lord's, where there are seats all the way round and no room for a parked car with a view, the watchers congregate in particular favoured spots. A regular crew of cronies always gravitates to the Long Room or the Tavern, and once there swaps audible anecdote and passes knowledgeable comment. It creates atmosphere.

At Canterbury, however, I felt as if I was at a point-to-point. Instead of congregating in sociable groups, spectators sat beside their Range Rovers with their wives and their labradors drinking gin and tonic from small plastic glasses and minding their own business. They came with their own fold-up chairs and their own picnics, and I was told by the man on the gate that before a big game there is an astounding ritual, like the start of a Silverstone Grand Prix, as members queue up for the best parking lots and then barge in when the gates open just like Ayrton Senna and Alain Prost jockeying for position on the first bend.

So I felt there was some justice in the smashed windscreen; however, there was compensation, and because this was cricket the compensation was rather charmingly organised. The ball was autographed by Ritchie and presented to the car's owner as a souvenir of the occasion. Very British.

I went on the August Bank Holiday, and it was noticeable that this was a holiday occasion in a new and rather saddening sense: at the Nackington Road end there is an old iron stand, built in the late 1850s and now given a plate glass face-lift in order to accommodate sixteen executive boxes. It is named after Leslie Ames, one of that great line of Kentish wicketkeeper-batsmen, and on August Bank Holiday it was virtually empty. No dark suits. No business lunch. I can only suppose they were all off playing golf. Clearly there is no demand for an executive cricket-watching facility on a bank holiday. There is obviously no point in inviting businessmen to the cricket unless it gives them an excuse to get out of the office.

Otherwise it was a good crowd. Despite the threat of impending rail strike the train was full of tourists and trippers heading for the Kent coast. From the window you could see apples and hops and oast-houses and the cathedral at Rochester. Canterbury's cathedral is older and grander, of course, but the cricket ground is out on the Old Dover Road, away from the city centre. The quickest way is to turn right out of the station and walk along the ring road, but that is deadly dull and it doesn't take much longer to cross over and walk the old city wall as far as a roundabout, where you cut off and walk past Oaten Hill and Nunnery Fields and realise you are getting warm when you reach the Bat and Ball pub and Cowdrey Place.

The ground is at its absolute best during the famous cricket week, when there are tents and bunting and bands. There is still an office at Canterbury called 'The Week Office', the name dating from the days when the county was itinerant and had a series of offices wherever they played one of their 'weeks'. Nowadays it is the home of the public address system.

The first thing a visitor should do is to turn left inside the ground and pay his or her respects at the two memorials. One is to Colin Blythe and the other to Fuller Pilch. Pilch's used to be in St Stephen's Church and has a wonderfully stiff upper lip sort of inscription which says: 'This monument is erected to the memory of Fuller Pilch by upwards of two hundred friends to mark their admiration of his skill as a cricketer and his worth as a man.' It adds that from 1836 to 1854 he was 'the best batsman known to cricket before the advent of W. G. Grace'. From 1847 to 1862 he was the Kent groundsman. He batted in a black top hat, was landlord of the Saracen's Head, and his snuff-box is in the pavilion.

There was a sad bunch of carnations at the foot of Blythe's memorial which says that he was 'unsurpassed among the famous bowlers of the period and beloved by his fellow cricketers'. In the fifteen years before the Great War he took 2,210 wickets at under seventeen apiece. The Blythe pavilion memento is more macabre. It is his wallet, shredded by the shrapnel which killed him at Ypres in 1917. He was just thirty-eight years old.

They are keen on their history at Canterbury and, thanks to their two honorary curators, E. W. Swanton and Chris Taylor (who can usually be found in the 'Week Office'), they have a photograph on the dining-room wall of every man who has won his county cap. Chris, who has been watching cricket at Canterbury since 1928 when he was eight years old, prides himself on having a newly capped player's picture on the wall almost as soon as the captain has presented him with his hat. For this Australian match a seriously depleted side were obliged to field their cricket manager and former player, Brian Luckhurst. Luckhurst was supposed to have retired almost ten years earlier but already Chris Taylor had amended the dates to take account of this unexpected curtain call. 'Career under review' it said under his picture.

The ground's most famous feature is the tree, though not everyone seems to realise this. The artist commissioned to paint a picture of the ground for 'Project '85', which involves the building of the first brand new stand since 1926, managed to put the celebrated lime behind the boundary and off the field of play. Presumably when he got home and looked at his sketches he assumed that he had been hallucinating. After the limited edition of prints had been produced the tree was repainted on each one by hand!

The consensus is that the tree is a lime and about two hundred years old. The tree surgeons apparently say that it is good for another seventy, but if it did have to be felled you can bet your life the Kent marketing experts would make the most of it. The 'Project '85' leaflet carries an announcement about the tree which so perfectly captures one facet of modern county cricket that I feel it is worth reproducing virtually in full. It comes under a small drawing of the tree together with another of a bat and wicket in a glass case, and it reads thus:

'There is only one tree in the world that is within the boundary of a first-class cricket ground. Yes, you're right – the famous lime tree at the St Lawrence Ground, Canterbury. Loved by generations, this common lime has presided over some 200 years of cricketing history. Now you can own a piece of this famous tree. For Project '85 the Kent County Cricket Club has arranged for a small number of miniature sets of stumps, bails and bats to be made from boughs of the St Lawrence lime, which were saved when the tree was pollarded in 1980.

'Each commemorative set will be hand made, numbered and mounted under a protective glass covering. For just £260 you can own a piece of unique cricketing history. To reserve your set apply to: the Secretary, Kent County Cricket Club, St Lawrence Ground, Canterbury, Kent, England, enclosing your cheque.'

I suppose I am prissy to be depressed by this and to find my only marginal consolation in the fact that the souvenir is not described as 'prestigious'. The new stand should provide additional income of £50,000 a year, much of it from the new 'Executive Club with viewing balcony'.

Brian Fitch – Groundsman

This is hard lines on the tree which deserves – I feel – a more romantic fate. On the morning I went to Canterbury *The Times* printed a photograph of Alan Border leaning against the tree while allegedly fielding. He looked quite pastoral. I was also told that Kent members are entitled, after cremation, to be scattered around the tree. After rain or a heavy dew the grass thereabouts is alleged to be a quite different colour, and the St Lawrence Ground joke is that these are the only non-combatants allowed on to the field of play actually during a match.

You can still see the cathedral from the boundary near the tree, although this is something which old stagers had told me was no longer possible. Certainly the cathedral in no sense dominates or even overlooks the ground. Canterbury is one of those places where the most important features are the pavilion and stands themselves. Those and the cars.

The cricketer that senior Kentings like Chris Taylor remember with the greatest awe is nearly always Frank Woolley. It seems sad that such an elegant carefree batsman should be commemorated with such a prosaic grandstand. 'He could play fast bowling with a walking stick,' said Mr Taylor, recalling Woolley against Larwood and Voce. According to the honorary curator, Woolley's greatest virtue (though statistically his greatest vice) was his habit of getting out in the nineties.

Nevertheless, apart from the war years, Woolley scored over a thousand runs for Kent every year from 1907 until 1935. He caught 773 catches, too, as well as taking 1,680 wickets. In youth and age Woolley always managed to look stylish and quixotic. 'Easy to watch, difficult to bowl to, and impossible to write about' was R. C. Robertson-Glasgow's pithy verdict. He hit his highest Kent score, 270, on the St Lawrence Ground against Middlesex in 1923, but the achievements I would most like to have witnessed took place elsewhere. In 1909, the year he first played for England, he and Arthur Fielder put on 235 for the last wicket against Worcester. They put on the first 119 in the last hour of the second day and 116 in the first hour of the third. When they started they were forty short of Worcester's 360. When they had finished they were so far ahead they went on to win by an innings. Four years later he and Colin Blythe bowled Warwickshire out for 16 in forty-three minutes. They both took five for eight.

Kent is a grand cricketing county, replete with history and great names. Five Kent cricketers have captained England: I saw one of them, Mike Denness, wandering rather diffidently round the outfield. The earliest of his predecessors was Lord Harris, a much more ebullient figure, even though Denness had a higher batting average. There is a wonderful picture of Lord Harris taking strike, which I particularly enjoyed because there had been a lot of frothing on the part of the tetchier older guard of cricket writers and supporters about cricketers' kits. The general drift was that it was deeply shocking that modern cricketers didn't wear the proper county cap. The retired major school of thought took great exception to these damned floppy white sun-hat things Clive Lloyd brought over from the Caribbean. Yet here was Lord Harris, circa 1880, wearing just such a hat with a snap brim and a pale blue ribbon, together with a bow tie, a fine moustache and an expression of infinite superiority. Best of all, he is holding his bat about two feet off the ground in much the way that Graham Gooch waits for the bowler. That too aroused great ire among the purists, who thought it new-fangled. Some cricket 'purists' would think lob bowling new-fangled.

After Harris came Ivo Bligh. Then Percy Chapman, who won six Tests in succession against Australia. Then Colin Cowdrey, most famous of all Kent moderns. Cowdrey is one of four Kent trustees; his son Chris is the present county captain; and his bat is in the pavilion. Cowdrey was the hero of the last great Kent victory over the Australians in 1975. Set to make 354 at more than a run a minute, Cowdrey brought them home with 151 not out.

That was Kent's sixth victory over the Australians, but there was never a hope of a repetition in the summer of '85. 'Bit of a massacre,' I heard one member mutter into his gin. 'Well, it's a stupid side to put out,' said the second member, gazing thoughtfully at the 46-year-old Luckhurst. 'Tomorrow will be a bit of a waste of time.' And it was.

Odd how little things can colour your view of a place. There was a small group of drunks standing by the public seats to the right of the Woolley stand. They drank beer and also passed around what looked like a bottle of rum. By soccer standards they were entirely harmless, but their incessant boorish shouts were, well, boorish. When Jeff Thomson came in to bat they barracked, only they weren't sober or clever enough to barrack. They just belched out a sort of porcine 'Oi, Oi, Oi' noise. And it *was* irritating that the Kent team seemed so feeble; and that somehow it didn't seem to be a very important occasion. And I didn't like that car park feel.

Yet there was Derek Underwood wheeling away; and Border and Ritchie did bat beautifully; and the Canterbury cricket week has been delighting Kentish crowds since 1842; and it *is* a unique tree. . . .

CANNONBALL CRICKET, HOUNSLOW

*'It's Fast! It's Fun!
It's for Everyone!'*

As far as cricket is concerned I think I may have seen the future. I found it in a converted warehouse in Hounslow, and it works. The surroundings are hardly picturesque. Jets bound for Heathrow thunder overhead only seconds, surely, from touchdown. There is a certain leafiness about Hounslow Heath, but that is several minutes' walk away. Green Lane, down which you drive after leaving the Staines Road, also sounds the sort of place for a cricket pitch, but Tamian Way where the future lies is wall to wall concrete and high mesh fencing. This is twentieth-century industrial estate. Dispiriting desert.

Nevertheless this is a place endorsed by David Gower, the England captain himself, who grins out of a coloured brochure and invites everyone to 'come and see us for a free trial game.' This is the home of Cannonball Cricket – 'It's Fast! It's Fun! – It's For Everyone!' It was a warehouse, but now it is 25,000 square feet of indoor cricket 'courts' – six of them, complete with specially designed wickets that bend in any direction and electronic scoreboards for each court.

Its popularity is growing so fast that any claim made in this book will be out of date by the time it is published (unless I am hopelessly wrong and the whole thing has gone bust). I dare say to the purist it isn't cricket. But it is played with the same shots and the same bowling action and the same bat. The advantages are that it is not susceptible to rain or bad light or any of the other vicissitudes of the English summer, and it is all over in about an hour and a half. And, best of all, everyone has to bowl two eight-ball overs and bat for four. No way can you languish in the deep with never a catch to drop, never a ball to bowl and never an innings to play.

This is a genuine team game.

When I first went to Cannonball it was midday and the place was deserted except for Colin Lumley who runs it. Lumley is a young Australian Real Tennis professional. The first year he came here he was quite surprised to find that there were no indoor cricket courts in the UK. The second time he came he was still more surprised. And the third time he was so astounded that he decided to remedy the deficiency himself. In Australia there are thirty-five such 'centres' in Melbourne alone; more than two hundred nationwide.

That first day Lumley explained the rules, which like Real Tennis rules sound incredibly complicated off court but become pleasantly logical once you actually start to play. Then he bowled me a few. The ball is a lawn tennis ball in a leather case. Heavy enough to give you a sense of satisfaction if you hit it hard in the meat of the bat; not so heavy that it hurts you if it hits you in the middle. It was the first time I had been seriously bowled at since 1965, when I opened the innings

against Great Tew and was out first ball. For the first time in over twenty years I thought this might be my game after all.

I understood the principle of the thing: sixteen overs a side between two eight-man teams; taut netting off which the ball rebounds to give catches; automatic runs depending on where exactly you hit it; minus five every time you are out, and so on.

A few nights later I came back to see the real McCoy. Every court – rather bigger than a Lawn Tennis court but smaller than a Real one – was occupied. The leagues were already over-subscribed and I was watching a Real Tennis eight called the Under Arms. Their motto, the work I suspected of the assistant Hampton Court professional Lachlan Deuchar, was 'We're the pits'. They were all Real Tennis players – Deuchar; his boss Chris Ronaldson, the world champion; David Johnson, the pro from Queen's, wearing a Mumm champagne T-shirt; David Cull, the Lord's pro; Julian Snow and Thane Warburg, two of the leading amateurs, and others.

They were up against a team of tough-looking Pakistanis from Dulwich or thereabouts, and they lost. It was an endlessly fluctuating contest. Just as the Under Arms seemed to be on top the Pakistanis would hit a couple of sixes (full-toss into the back netting); just as David Johnson seemed to have the measure of the other side's bowling he would serve up a couple of catches and there would be ten less on the board. In the end Deuchar and Ronaldson had too many runs to make, slogged away in a vain pursuit, and paid the price.

You don't even need a box, but each batsman must wear one protective glove. 'The umpire shall determine if dress is unacceptable for play.' If so, you won't be allowed on court. And if you're not wearing a matching team shirt, then it's minus five.

It was very noisy on court that night. The appeals were magnified by the echo in the huge warehouse. The atmosphere was exuberant – more like baseball than cricket.

'It's not a spectator sport,' said Colin Lumley. 'That's the point. It's meant to be fun to play.'

Not cricket. But, 'It's Fast! It's Fun! It's For Everyone!'

Some of the best players, says Lumley, have never played cricket. Even those who have are not necessarily any good. He wants it to be called simply 'Cannonball', with all reference to the ancient outdoor game on grass to be eliminated. He could be right. At all events the full colour sheet offering the free trial under the David Gower seal of approval does not mention the word cricket once. Instead it says, 'CBC: A whole new ball game.'

Maybe so.

TAUNTON

*'If you can see
the Quantocks,
it means rain;
if not, it's
raining already'*

It was R. C. 'Crusoe' Robertson-Glasgow, best so far of the distinguished company of Somerset cricket writers, who said that 'if you wanted to know Taunton, you walked round it with Sam Woods on a summer morning before the match.' Sam, best so far in a distinguished company of Somerset cricket characters and all-rounders, was, in Crusoe's words, 'Somerset's godfather'. There is a picture of him in the new, blood brick pavilion at Taunton: an enormous, jovial man, sitting rather far back on a small donkey. The caption does not explain the picture at all. C. B. Fry told Robertson-Glasgow that Sam, when a young man, 'was the finest build of an athlete stripped that he ever saw.' And: 'He was convivial; too convivial, some thought; but I could never see that it mattered.'

I was far too young to see Sammy Woods. Even Robertson-Glasgow only saw him 'trundling a few down, in waistcoat and watch-chain when he was fifty-two.' I was too young to see Robertson-Glasgow, even though he played on my prep school ground at Bishops Lydeard in the days when it was owned by Sir Denis Boles. While placing a field he once surprised his host, then on the boundary in earnest confabulation with his butler, by shouting at him, 'Up a bit, Boles.' Jack MacBryan the Somerset batsman was so amused at this lèse-baronetcy that he had to sit down on the grass and laugh.

My first glimpse of Somerset was in the summer of 1957 when they played the West Indies. It was the first time I had actually been on the Taunton ground, though the maroon coaches from Berry Brothers passed by every Thursday when we went swimming at Taunton Baths. My mother's family came from Martock, where the vicar was Crusoe's great-uncle, Prebendary A. P. Wickham, who kept wicket when W. G. Grace scored his hundredth hundred, 288, for Gloucestershire against Somerset. Wickham told his great-nephew that only five balls passed the doctor's bat in the entire innings. Much the same is said of Archie Maclaren's 424. Prebendary Wickham was behind the stumps then, too.

I mention all this to indicate that as far as Somerset cricket and the Taunton ground are concerned I am one of nature's fogeys. I want no changes at the Taunton ground, because it is a place I knew as a child. My Somerset cricket links go back way beyond my birth, and when I first lived in the county they were easily the worst team in the championship. *Wisden* said 'general slackness' was their greatest problem, and 'it was no surprise when they finished bottom.'

When I visited Taunton at the fag end of the summer of 1985 they were again clearly about to finish last in the championship, and yet this time it was a matter for almost universal surprise. With Ian

Botham as skipper, and Garner to help him with the bowling and Richards to help him with the batting, how could they fail? Modern Somerset teams are seldom underdogs. In the old days they nearly always were.

If Sammy Woods had been alive he would have found not only the team but much of town and ground unrecognisable. I am not sure I would have enjoyed walking round Taunton with Sammy Woods in the summer of 1985. Were it not for the fact that he seems to have been incorrigibly cheerful, I am not sure he would either.

What would Sammy have made of the two Tandoori Restaurants on the short walk from railway station to ground, or the Microwave Oven Centre or the Video Shop or 'West Country Acquatics'? Why had someone written, on the side of the bridge that crosses the River Tone, 'Where are the Taunton Trendy Boys?' What could it mean?

And yet the important fixed points remain. The Quantocks still straggle away towards Minehead. Sam Woods used to hide bottles of beer about those hills, producing them with a flourish when his walking companions got thirsty. Maybe some of them are still there. St James's church, hard by the old pavilion, still leads the little flotilla of three church towers angled away to the south-east. But here too there have been changes. The memorial tablets to the Yea family are still there, including the one to the Colonel Yea who died leading his men at the siege of Sevastopol. (He was mentioned in Raglan's dispatches.) But there is carpet on the floor and in the Church Magazine the editorial, under a photo of a smiling priest, is headed 'Malcolm Writes'. One wonders whether this is where the Taunton trendy boys are to be found, and why Auberon Waugh, who lives just up the road in Combe Florey, has not made a target of the Rev. Malcolm.

At the entrance to the ground are Jack White Gates, in memory of another great Somerset cricketer. Unlike so many of the Somerset names, Jack White was a local farmer and not an import. Sometimes, on our way to the swimming baths in the fifties, our prep school bus used to get stuck behind his hay lorry. He didn't play for England until he was thirty-seven, then went to Australia and took four for seven in six overs in the first Test, following with a match-winning thirteen in 124 overs at Adelaide. It was very hot. 'I used a few shirts and several whisky and sodas,' he said.

It wasn't like that this time in Taunton. Proper parky it was, and the rain had got under the covers round the square. Our gallant band of spectators were more optimistic than the players. Joel Garner was in jeans and Viv was in civvies too. Umpires Oslear and Hampshire kept announcing pitch inspections and spent long depressing moments with Vic Marks, the home skipper, and John Barclay of Sussex, peering at the damp around the square.

It was a shock seeing the ground for the first time since 1976. That year I went there on Ascension Day with Christopher Hollis, sometime

MP, poet, publisher and villain of that famous prep school match between Horris Hill and Summer Fields. It was the first time either of us had seen Botham. He came in when Somerset were 70 for five against the West Indies, with Wayne Daniel and Andy Roberts bowling very nastily. He wasn't in very long, but made 56, including a six over long-stop, and 48 of them in boundaries. It was the fearlessness and the joie de vivre which were so attractive. He seemed to be absolutely in the tradition of Woods and Earle and Wellard and the great Gimblett, who hit that extraordinary maiden century in his first ever match at Frome and took sixty-three minutes over it.

The Taunton ground in 1976 was as my aunts and great-aunts remembered it. Rickety old pavilion up at the St James's End, screens and a few seats down the other, where the river was an invitation to the big hitter. But now all is changed. Old pavilion condemned unfit for use, new pavilion down by the Tone: result unrecognisable.

I felt slightly as I did when I went back to my old college only a year after going down and found that my staircase had been bulldozed and replaced by a piece of sixties brutalism. Even where old institutions had survived I was reminded of time's passage. 'Follow Somerset County Cricket Club with Berry's Executive Coaches' said one hoarding. In the good old days there were just the two Berry buses. Old Mr Berry drove the pre-war charabanc and young Mr Berry – bit of a Brylcreem boy – drove the state of the art brand new coach. That was how we got to St Dunstan's and St Peter's at Weston-Super-Mare, struggling up Cothelstone Hill and over the Quantocks in our blue

blazers. 'Executive Coaches' indeed. What would the headmaster, Randall Hoyle, have said?

It is the new pavilion which has most transformed the place. Apart from that dreaded architect's brick it is the most successful of all the new pavilions in appearance: deep balconies, high roof, clock in the middle, and a good view of the churches. I heard complaints that it looks straight into the afternoon sun. Also it is at an angle to the wicket whereas the old one was – *is*, unless very recently demolished – right behind the bowler's arm.

Inside it is light and spacious and manages to seem prosperous. Although Somerset have still to win the championship, they have been more successful in one-day competition and in 1979 carried off both the Gillette and John Player League trophies. Despite being a largely rural county they have a membership of around six thousand, including well over five hundred from Devon. As the club was founded in the Devon town of Sidmouth in 1875 after a match between the Gentlemen of the two counties, there is an appropriateness about this, and I was pleased to see a note in the pavilion which said, 'Are you a Somerset Supporter? Do you live in Devon? Travel by Coach from Okehampton.'

Not only is there a supporters club, there is also something called the Somerset Wyverns which is an organisation of expatriate Somerset men under the presidency of Jeffrey Archer. (One way or another Somerset has become very showbiz in recent years – a bit like Fulham in the days of Johnny Haynes and Jimmy 'the Rabbi' Hill.) I was approached on their behalf at Arundel by the chairman Royse Riddell and am now a member and possessor of the club tie, a vivid maroon number with a gold Wyvern – though purists apparently insist that it is a Wessex Dragon and not a Wyvern at all. I always thought they were one and the same. I am not sure about belonging to a club whose president is Jeffrey Archer, although I admit his Somerset links – he was at school at the Somerset Wellington – seem stronger than mine; but we are a good cause. Last year we gave the county a new Motomop. It cost five hundred pounds.

There are some new pictures in the pavilion, notably of the great Vivian Richards. Rather good ones. He looks like a black Mr Punch, though no picture can quite convey the irresistible quality of Richards on song. The earlier team pictures have a more raffish air about them than at any other county I found. Look at Sammy Woods in 1890 in his trilby, or Sir H. Ponsonby Fane with boater, frock coat, cane and rosette. Upstairs in the committee room are one or two old scorecards. There are two from 1925. One is of the Essex match when Jack Daniel, the Somerset skipper, made 174 in one innings and 108 in the other. He was forty-six at the time. The other is of the game when Jack Hobbs equalled and then surpassed Dr Grace's record of 126 centuries by also scoring a century in each innings. Robertson-Glasgow took one for 144 in the first and nought for 42 in the second innings. But, as always, he described the occasion beautifully. Hobbs had been on the brink of the record for weeks.

'It was a Saturday, and the rubicund face of Mr Secretary Davey smiled to its limit as he saw the crowds roll in, but turned a little paler as he watched the motion-picture experts, with their impedimenta, climb on to the tin roof of the old pavilion. Most of the West Country, and several segments of London S.E., seemed to be present; clergymen, schoolboys, cockneys, farmers, Jack White's father on his favourite bench, and the still excited but visibly tiring cohort from Fleet Street. Even the ladies, without whom all cricket matches grow dull, forbore to discuss husbands and the contents of shop-windows, and joined in the single question – "Will he do it?"'

He did.

Whatever one's views on the new pavilion, it is clear that there are plenty of Somerset people with a proper respect for the past and its heroes. J. Archer has presented the club with a Spy picture of Lionel Palairet who, with H. T. Hewett, put on 346 for the first wicket against Yorkshire here in 1892. Yeovil Town Football Club presented a silver salver in recognition of the triumphs of 1979 ('Congratulations and our thanks for putting Somerset sport on the map'); and there is a red and gold Wyvern embroidered by Jack MacBryan of Somerset and England, the same who had to sit on the grass and laugh at Robertson-Glasgow when he said, 'Up a bit, Boles.' MacBryan did the embroidery in his ninetieth year.

There has been some rowdyism in recent years, for which there are several explanations: a lot of one-day success; an excess of scrumpy; no local league soccer as an alternative. As a result there are fierce signs up saying that the club reserves the right to remove anyone from the ground – member or not – if he doesn't comply with the rules. That includes using obscene language. And they also 'reserve the right to search persons entering the ground and to confiscate any intoxicating liquor found.'

I sat on a wooden bench by a bar which I think, though I may be mistaken, was reserved for the use of vice-presidents, and drank a pint of Dry Blackthorn Cider matured hard by in Norton Fitzwarren. It was too quiet a day to have my drink confiscated. A fly landed in the cider and drowned at once. A woman in a blue sweater asked, amazingly, if Somerset had ever come bottom of the championship before. Another spectator said, 'Not since Brian Close was here.' I stifled an urge to tell them about the early fifties, and the woman went to sleep in a deck chair.

Out on the square the umpires and captains were peering at the turf and scuffing their shoes about. I walked out on to the pitch to have a look for myself and was joined by a vice-president of the club, a structural engineer from a village near Yeovil. He played a lot of village cricket. If it had been us, we agreed, we would have played. 'My old aunt used to say,' he said, '"If you can see the Quantocks it means rain, and if you can't see them then it's raining already."' I said I'd had an old aunt in Creech St Michael and that was the sort of thing I would expect her to say too. She was a very keen cricket supporter. 'What niggles me,' said my friend, who was resigned to having taken a day off without play, 'is that it costs forty-three pounds a year to be a vice-president.' He didn't think the players and umpires remembered that often enough.

Since 1882 Somerset have played more than five hundred matches on this ground. After a hundred and two years the record was: Won 133, Drawn 187, Lost 199, Tied 1; Abandoned 3. That's not such a bad record, and yet Somerset, I feel, has less to do with facts and figures than any other county. The inevitable Crusoe wrote: 'In the long view it is not the arithmetical performances of this or that player, not merely the times of success and failure that strike the historian of Somerset cricket. It is rather the spirit – the spirit which win or lose has always been a happy compound of humour and independence.'

I have an uneasy feeling that perhaps that is not quite as true as it was and that too much showbiz and success has not altogether improved the character of Somerset cricket. Even so, and whatever the changes, I can never visit the Taunton ground without remembering the original Berry bus and Randall Hoyle in his Hawks tie and my aunts and Harold Gimblett and Bill Alley and the unfortunately named fast bowler Lobb and, most of all, the day I went with Christopher Hollis and we got that first marvellous glimpse of Botham batting.

But I do regret not seeing Woods. On one occasion he took all ten wickets after a huge breakfast of lobsters and beer; three times he hit a hundred before lunch; and he won that great match after Somerset had been given first-class status in 1891. It was against Surrey. And it was at Taunton. Woods was due to bowl the last ball of the match at the Surrey number eleven, Sharpe. Just before he bowled, the other batsman said to Sammy: 'Keeps his end up well for a man with one eye, eh?' Woods asked which one and, on being told the left, bowled 'my first round-arm ball of my life, and hit his off-stump.'

'Had I not had the information,' he said, 'we wouldn't have won.' He considered this was the day that 'made' Somerset cricket. 'Our spectators went barmy,' he said, 'flung their hats in the air and hit each other about.'

Taunton's ghosts are the most genial I can think of; and they and my own personal links and memories mean that I shall always carp at the changes but always forgive. Whatever they do to it; whether or not there are trendy boys in the executive boxes, or the Quantocks are visible, or the players are as merry as they used to be, it will always be a special place, especially for those who like the idea of flinging their hats in the air and hitting each other about.

THE OVAL

*'Gower and Border
weren't even born
when Hutton's team
beat Hassett's'*

Life is maddeningly full of either/ors. You can't be Oxford *and* Cambridge. You have to be either Everton or Liverpool. Sitting on the fence is Laodicean. 'So then,' as the Book of Revelation has it, 'because thou art luke-warm and neither cold nor hot, I will spue thee out of my mouth.' I feel like this about Lord's and the Oval. For a Londoner, at least, impartiality is not possible. Years ago I used to have coaching at Alf Gover's in-door school in Clapham; I now seem to have a Surrey postal address; I grew up in the years of the Surrey and Surridge ascendancy, when Bedser and Loader, Lock and Laker, May and Barrington and Subba Row carried all before them; but still I remain dubious about the county and its famous cricketing home.

Of course this is perverse. Gordon Ross, in his excellent little essay which Surrey use as their 'standard hand-out', demonstrates that Surrey cricket has a long and glorious history, though not always at the Oval. The first mention of Surrey cricket is actually at their second, barely used, home in Guildford. That was in 1598. In 1700 they were playing 'Ten Gentlemen on each side' on Clapham Common and for ten pounds a head each game. And Moulsey Hurst in Surrey was the scene of the first recorded leg before wicket. Surrey were playing 'Thirteen of England' and the Hon. J. Tufton was lbw to Wells.

The club was formally inaugurated on 18 October 1845 at the Horns Tavern in Kennington. The motion 'That a Surrey Club be now formed' was passed, according to Gordon Ross, 'amidst universal cheering' from the hundred or so club cricketers present. Kennington Oval was then a market garden surrounded by a hedge, and it was owned – as it still is – by the Duchy of Cornwall (hence Surrey's cap badge of Prince of Wales feathers and Prince of Wales 'Ich Dien' motto). The Duchy were quite happy for it to be turned over to a different use. The original lease was for thirty-one years at a hundred and twenty pounds per annum. The first of ten thousand turfs from Tooting was laid by Mr Turtle, who charged three hundred pounds. Nowadays the Duchy still profess to be keen that cricket should be played on their land for ever and a day. Yet they manifest their enthusiasm in a curious manner. The last lease was for thirty-four years. The new one, awaiting final signature at the time of writing, is for fifteen years. I think the Duke of Cornwall, aka the Prince of Wales, should put his mouth where his feathers are and give the club a thousand-year lease on a peppercorn rent. But then cricket was never really his game.

There have been stirring deeds there since 1845. The first Test match in England; the first loss of the Ashes; the immortal rearguard action of Hirst and Rhodes, when Hirst said, 'Wilfred, we'll get 'em in singles'; Hobbs's and Bradman's final Test innings; Hutton's 364 out of England's 903 for seven in 1938. Because it is the traditional venue of the final Test in every series, it tends to have a crucial significance, which Lord's with its second Test somehow lacks. Nor has its history been just cricket. The first FA Cup Final was played at the Oval between, wait for it, 'The Wanderers' and the Royal Engineers. The winter before last it was the scene of the deciding fixture in the series between the British and American ladies' lacrosse teams. And during the war it was supposed to be a POW camp, although it never held prisoners.

Neville Cardus has a famous story of the eve of the Second World War in the Long Room at Lord's when workmen came and took away the bust of W.G. It was then that Cardus realised things were getting serious. When I mentioned that story in a *Times* book review, I was sent a note by a Dr Philip Evans who was working at King's College Hospital in 1939. He had been in the States for two years and could not believe that war was a genuine possibility. Every day he went to work on the tram past the Oval. 'About three days before Chamberlain declared war I was looking from the upper deck down on the sacred turf of the Oval,' he told me, 'and I saw that two wide discs of it had been dug up for gun emplacements. I knew then that war was inevitable.' So the Oval is hallowed ground.

Despite this, I don't, if we are going to be absolutely honest, much care for the gasholders. Their correct corporate designation is 'The Kennington Holder Station' and they come under the aegis of the British Gas Corporation South Eastern Region. They have now fallen victim to the contemporary craze of advertising on every available public surface and have 'WONDERFUEL' in huge lettering on the side where the television cameras can pick them up. If you have only seen the ground on television you will be unprepared for the way those four great cylinders crowd and dominate the place. They are like creatures of H. G. Wells or John Wyndham, monsters about to devour the poor little Cricketers public house which crouches beneath them. Despite its name, the Cricketers is more of a music than a sporting pub. Indeed it says it is 'London's Premier Jazz House'. When I was there they were expecting all the best acts: Georgie Fame, George Melly, Hershey and the Twelve Bars, Eddie and the Hot Rods, even Juice on the Loose.

Apart from the gasholders and the pub, the main landmark is Archbishop Tenison's grammar school, endowed in 1685 but showing no evidence of seventeenth-century design. There is also a Church of England School, St Mark's, at the Vauxhall end. The perimeter, patrolled according to the warnings by Centuryon Guard Dogs, is surrounded by roads, one a main bus route, the other lazily residential. The residences are flats – most, if not all, owned by the GLC. They look characterless and rather mean.

Despite these frankly tacky South London environs Surrey cricket has just as often been characterised by elegance as obduracy. For every Roundhead Barrington there was a Cavalier May. Lord Dalmeny scored two centuries for them before the Great War. Percy Fender, who hit a hundred in 35 minutes, was obviously a player and captain of startling panache. In the Centenary Library, opened in 1980 by two non-Surrey men, Bobby Simpson and Colin Cowdrey, you can still see Fender's cap. It is under glass, next to the cigar case given to H. D. G. Leveson Gower by Mr 'Buns' Cartwright (an improbable souvenir).

Above all, of course, Surrey had Hobbs. Their gates are named after him – a fair tribute to a man who made more appearances and scored more runs for Surrey than anyone. He hit 144 Surrey centuries in all, and downstairs, close to Fender's cap and Leveson Gower's cigar case, is one of his bats. It has 'Old Style Handle' embossed on the blade just below the splice and underneath the Master has written, in wonderfully neat forward-sloping black not quite copperplate: 'I scored 37 and 100 with this bat in fifth "Test" match against Australia at Kennington Oval – August 1926. J. B. Hobbs.' Note the 'Kennington' and the inverted commas around Test.

When I took the family to see Somerset play the home team in a John Player League game they ran out of sandwiches. We got the last two and split them six ways. Also, foolishly, we sat just over the midwicket boundary, a silly place to be sitting when Botham and Richards are vying with each other in a race to see who can score most sixes. Balls to the right of us, balls to the left of us, balls in front of us, volley'd and thunder'd. Despite their new Trinidadian fast bowler, a Joel Garner clone called Tony Gray, the Surrey attack looked pretty plain. Under those circumstances, mind you, Bedser, Loader, Laker and Lock would be pressed to look penetrating. It reminded me of prep school, fielding at square leg when our bowlers were pitching short – the terrible realisation that you are a sitting target.

Immediately underneath us the long-suffering fielder, smiling ruefully under his chocolate brown Surrey cap, was David Ward, who earlier in the season scored a maiden hundred against Derby in a shade over two hours after being called up unexpectedly one lunchtime. He made 143 with seventeen fours, substituting for Trevor Jesty. Bucktoothed and vulnerable, Ward looked as apprehensive as the rest of us.

When you say, diffidently, to the Surrey secretary Ian Scott-Browne that the Oval isn't all it might be, he is apt to disarm the criticisms with even fiercer ones of his own. The umpires' changing-room, for instance. 'It's a disgrace,' he says. 'We hope to do something about it in the very near future.' The loos at the Vauxhall End. Indeed the whole of the Vauxhall end. Well yes, he will concede, the loos are a disgrace too and the stands aren't a lot better, but there's a million pounds in the kitty thanks to the appeal for the Kenny Barrington

sports centre and, 'given a fair wind', it will be built in the winter of 1986–87.

The trouble is that with a big old ground like the Oval the money gets eaten up in invisible improvements. They recently spent £28,000 on rewiring. The members couldn't see the new wires, of course, but if it hadn't been done there would have been a fire risk. The pavilion is a good building, sturdily constructed, but it is a hundred years old and sometimes the roof springs a leak and the plumbing gives out. Smaller county grounds don't have such enormous overheads.

By rights the ground really shouldn't be there. Despite the grottiness of the immediate surroundings it is only a stroll from Parliament and the Tate Gallery, not much further from the City of London. Those 9.8 acres must be worth millions to a property developer. And nowadays Kennington is about six miles from the nearest part of Surrey. 'I suppose you could say we're the South London Cricket Club,' says Scott-Browne, a touch morosely. About a dozen years ago the club contemplated moving out into the county proper, just as Essex did from Leyton, their East London ground. The idea never came to anything, however, and apart from four days' play at Guildford every year the First XI play all their games in London. The colts and seconds carry the banner around the county proper, but their elders and betters remain where they always have done.

They like to claim that the Oval is a very friendly place, which I take to be a discreet swipe at Lord's. The crude characterisation would have it that Lord's is north of the river, toffee-nosed and stand-offish, while the Oval is full of 'real people', calling spades spades and being sunny and welcoming to all and sundry. Or, as the author and Surrey enthusiast Richard Gordon puts it, 'Lord's is the cathedral of cricket, the Oval low church.' There is some truth in this. That Somerset Sunday I was wandering past the practice net, jammed in between the perimeter wall (there's half a mile of it – another thankless expense) and the stands at the Vauxhall end, when a voice called out a decently respectful 'Good afternoon, Mr Heald.' It was Greg, the captain of my son's school Under-13 side. And as a result my son, Alexander, spent part of the afternoon bowling in the nets at the Oval. I doubt that could happen at Lord's. He has bowled in the nets there as well, but by appointment. If you measure friendliness by informality then, yes, the Oval is certainly a friendly place.

'Surrey cricket,' wrote Cardus, 'from days historical, has been one of the major nurseries of the England XI. What a roll of honour could be composed to hang on the wall of the pavilion at the Oval: the Reads, Shuter, Lohmann, Abel, Brockwell, Richardson, Lockwood, Hayward, Crawford, Hobbs, Strudwick, Sandham, Fender, Jardine, May, Bedser ... the list could go on much longer, and I hope no reader will take me to task for important omissions.

'I fancy that, to this illustrious succession of names, will one day (and not in the far distant future) be added those of Barrington and Stewart. Both are batsmen capable of going a long way in the best company.'

The sage was writing in 1955. Right about Barrington, marginally less so about Stewart. Even so, Stewart scored more runs for Surrey (over 25,000), was captain from 1963-72, and is now the county's cricket manager. But no one would put him in the same class as Barrington. John Edrich, perhaps. He scored more runs for Surrey than anyone but Hobbs, Hayward and Sandham. But then Graham Roope scored more runs for Surrey than Peter May, and we are not going to claim, are we, that Roope was a better batsman than May? No we are not.

Difficult, sadly, to put many of the present team in that category. Butcher? Always attractive to watch but. ... Against Somerset he flattered but only to deceive. Tony Gray looks like the new Garner but he is Trinidad and West Indies, not a native 'transpontine'. Perhaps Medlycott, young cricketer of the year in 1983, will come good, but in 1985 he only played one championship match. He scored five. Of them all Monte Lynch, still barred from consideration by England, looks the likeliest. Only he responded that afternoon to the challenge of Richards and Botham. He too hit sixes and was unafraid. Whenever I have seen him he stands tall and attacks.

Otherwise the present Surrey team seem a bit ordinary – certainly when you compare them with the great teams of the past. Their ground, on the other hand, is legendary. Great deeds have been done here by great cricketers, and season after season it is the setting for the last act of the Test series; the final balcony speeches to the crowds below. For me the greatest moment of all was the Oval Test of 1953 – Coronation Year – which ended in a win and the Ashes regained on 19 August. I wasn't there in *fact*, but somehow over the years I have convinced myself that I was there in spirit. The 1985 climax was enjoyable, too, though it was salutary to realise that the present England captain was not even born when Hutton's team beat Hassett's.

The Oval is not my favourite ground, but it does have an enjoyable knockabout egalitarianism even at the top. Ian Scott-Browne, the secretary, says he has been a Surrey supporter since he 'climbed over the wall as a youngster'. Nowadays, he adds, 'I get awfully cross if I find them doing it.'

I take that with a pinch of salt. The Oval is, par excellence, the sort of ground where boys will always climb in over the wall; where any twelve-year-old can have a bowl in the nets if he feels so inclined; and where the aesthetics are irrevocably determined by those dirty great gasholders.

I know that it is physically south of the Thames, but there is something about this ground which always makes me feel that it actually belongs north of the Trent. Nowt wrong with that. But whatever its pedigree, Kennington simply isn't my idea of Surrey.

JESMOND

'Even in the rain it felt first-class'

It was the ubiquitous Winlaw who sent me to Jesmond. While I was researching this book Winlaw was really the only cricket writer I came to know. There are two sorts of cricket correspondent – the grand ones like Woodcock and Marlar who do Test matches and NatWest finals, and your jobbing journalist like Winlaw who is left with the universities or Zimbabwe or mid-week matches between struggling, unfashionable counties when there is a Test match in progress some-where else. Because I often went to grounds during that sort of match I bumped into Winlaw several times and came to regard him as some-thing of a talisman, a beaming figure strolling round the boundary with a choc ice in one hand. I felt he brought me good luck. Seeing Winlaw was like seeing a second magpie.

It was at Leicester near the public seats by the car park end, hard by a dozing pensioner, that Winlaw said I must go to Close House, Corbridge, in Northumberland. Winlaw had played there against a team called the Northumberland Wanderers and the chap I should get in touch with was a man called Craig, who used to play for Winch-ester. Useful cricketer, Craig. Good enough to play minor county cricket for Northumberland. Winlaw rated the Close House ground as one of the prettiest in England.

I phoned Craig soon afterwards, and he seemed a bit dubious about Close House. It was run by the Newcastle University people these days and didn't get a lot of cricket. Yes, it was very beautiful, but the house was empty. It was, he implied, a bit sad, an echo of the leisured, moneyed past. But I was doing Jesmond, wasn't I?

'Jesmond?' I echoed, rather foolishly.

For a minute or two he extolled the virtues of Jesmond, headquart-ers of Northumberland cricket. All the pros loved coming there, he said, it was just like a Test ground with a proper pavilion and seating all the way round, and good wickets. In a week or so England were playing the Rest of the World there. I really ought to come.

I have to admit that what really sold me on Jesmond was not the cricket but the Real Tennis. There is a court there – one of fewer than twenty in the entire county – and when I mentioned this to Craig he said that he was one of the very few serious playing members. We agreed that we would play a game together and then he would take me over to look at the cricket ground.

It was mid-August when I drove up the motorway from the family's holiday home in the Yorkshire Dales. By the time we reached the outskirts of Newcastle the sky had turned an ominous purple and we made the mistake of crossing under the Tyne through the tunnel in-stead of going into the centre of town over the bridge. Jesmond is the

smart, mainly Victorian suburb to the north of Newcastle. It feels leafy and prosperous, as you'd expect of a place with a Real Tennis court and the county cricket ground.

The tennis court turned out to be in wonderfully good order, though peculiar because it is shared with a badminton club. Before playing we had to remove the badminton nets and put up our own. The floor is also marked for badminton, which is a little confusing at first. Craig, who turned out to be a solicitor called Nick, beat me comprehensively over three sets, and by the time we got outside the purple sky had unleashed a rainstorm of tropical proportions. We drove hurriedly to the lawn tennis club, Northumberland's answer to Queen's, with grandstand, comfortable club house and what looked like a large number of very good grass courts fast disappearing under water.

A beer later we adjourned to the cricket ground, less than five minutes' drive away, tucked down a side road. There should have been a club match in progress, but the scene in the pavilion was the depressingly familiar one of disconsolate players staring bleakly out at puddles and covers. There obviously wasn't going to be any play today and, worse still, I was seeing the ground under the least attractive conditions imaginable.

Even so I was impressed. Even in the storm it felt more like a first-class ground than some of those which actually enjoy that status. Its most severe drawback, as John Farmer, Northumberland's assistant secretary pointed out, was that the straight boundary is a good twenty yards short. 'Not a lot we can do about that,' he said. 'There's a road one end and consecrated ground the other.' If you're batting at the Osborne Road end at Jesmond you don't have to be Botham to find it quite easy to loft a six over the bowler's head into the cemetery.

It feels pleasantly snug, just as Nick Craig had suggested, like a Test ground in miniature, with seats all the way round and a pavilion with bar and restaurant, clock and balcony, built in 1967, which would certainly pass muster if it was transported to Hove, say, or even Headingley. On a big match day they can cram in three and a half thousand.

And they do get big matches. A local travel agency, Callers-Pegasus, sponsored a couple of one-day matches between an England XI and a Rest of the World XI, a 'festival' managed for the fifth successive year by Frank Twiselton, who used to be chairman of Gloucester. There's an element of 'Golden Oldie' about the teams, but not that much. Of the 'England' side in 1985 only Willis was not playing Test cricket or on the fringe of it. True, one or two like Fowler were suffering from 'loss of form' (as perplexing an affliction as 'writer's block' and not dissimilar), but this is not a bad team: Fowler, Moxon, Gatting, Lamb, Willey, Downton, Emburey, Edmonds, Allott, Willis and Cowans. 'The Rest' has a slightly more superannuated air about it, but if I lived in Morpeth or Hexham I think I'd have come in to have a look at them. Their team reads: Barlow (Eddie from South Africa), Richardson (Richie from the West Indies), Hookes, Greg Chappell, Kallicharran, Clive Lloyd, Wasim Raja, Roger Harper, Engineer, Holding and Rackemann.

Other matches stir the blood too. I'm not certain I'd be there for the average championship game, even for a local Derby like the Durham match, but every so often they qualify for the NatWest Cup. In 1984, for instance, they played Middlesex at Jesmond in the first round. Middlesex batted first and Northumberland had five of them out for 84. Four of them – Barlow, Gatting, Butcher and Downton – were Test players, and the other, Wilf Slack, very nearly one. It didn't last, alas, and Northumberland lost in the end by sixty runs.

It is a much used ground and many of its matches are less exalted than these. The 'Club and Ground' play all levels of League cricket. Alnwick and Morpeth and Ashington, Tynedale and Percy Main and Benwell Hill all feature on the official fixture list. Nick Craig, who plays for Benwell Hill, says the Northumberland League is not to be sneezed at. Not long ago he survived twenty-seven overs, scoring twelve, against the fast bowling of a lithe West Indian named Courtenay Walsh, the same man I saw skittling Australians for Gloucestershire a few weeks earlier. Craig says the dour, competitive struggles of the League have quite ruined southern-style country house cricket for him.

Truth to tell, though, he has always inclined to the gritty school of batsmanship. Read Geoffrey Moorhouse's *The Best Loved Game* for an account of Craig prodding away for Northumberland in a typical minor county match. Craig said someone read out the whole droll account at a cricket dinner one night and ruined his meal. It was, he conceded, quite accurate and very funny, but Moorhouse could expect to receive a stiff letter from his firm when he had time to draft one. And the locals are a bit sceptical about Wykhamists. 'Listen to this,' said one cricketer at a social after Craig's first game in the League. 'I've got someone here makes Prince Charles sound like a Geordie.'

The club was founded in 1895, and there was cricket played at Jesmond for a long time before that. In 1985, between 22 May and 12 August Jesmond staged fifty-one days of 'Club and Ground' cricket, eight of county, and eight of such 'one-offs' as the Festival games. There were only ten free days in all that time. Enthusiasm therefore runs high and yet it is a remote outpost. Plans to amalgamate with Durham and apply for first-class status foundered mainly because the costs were prohibitive but also because county cricketers would not regularly travel so far to earn their living. The Tresurer's Report concluded: 'There cannot be widespread optimism about 1985.' My impression is that there has never been widespread optimism about Northumberland cricket, but it bats on regardless out there on the boundary beyond long-off, in one of the few suburbs anywhere with a working Real Tennis court and a cemetery round two sides of the County Ground.

SOUTHAMPTON

*'Most typical of the
county grounds –
not too posh, red-brick,
pretty or run down'*

I was looking forward to Southampton because the Hampshire County Ground was celebrating its centenary. Mr James, the club secretary, in his final year of office, told me there would be 'modest celebrations', centred on the Australian match in June, and suggested I might like to come down a little later when the fuss had died down. The original opening, according to John Arlott, that celebrated old Hampshire hand, now in voluntary exile in the Channel Islands, was performed on 9 May 1885 over lunch. Lord Northesk, the president of the club, was in the chair and afterwards there was a Grand Bazaar opened by the Countess. The present Earl appears not to have any connection with the county. He lives on the Isle of Man and is an authority on Charolais cattle.

There was no match on the ground until five weeks after the lunch, when MCC came down. They out-gunned the county by two Majors (Wallace and Booth) to one (Fellowes), although Hampshire opened with a Bonham Carter. The county's undoing was not a Major but a real Gunn, William, the Nottingham opening bat who bowled unchanged through both innings and took eleven for 85. Hampshire lost by an innings.

Under Mark Nicholas, the young captain of the England B side, the present team are a stronger proposition. In fact, if there was a prize for the most generally successful side in 1985, Hampshire would probably have won it. Yet it went down as a season of near misses. They were just pipped for the championship and just lost to Essex in the semi-finals of the NatWest. They made the quarter-finals of the Benson and Hedges and were third in the John Player League. Ever since I can remember they have had attractive foreign opening batsmen down in Southampton. For almost twenty years from 1953, when I first took a serious interest in cricket, it was the West Indian Roy Marshall, then came the South African Barry Richards, and finally the West Indian Gordon Greenidge. I'd as soon watch Greenidge in full flow as anyone now playing. They lean heavily on him and on his compatriot Malcolm Marshall, but there are some good Englishmen there too these days.

I was looking forward to seeing a crucial game in the closing stages of the championship when I was unexpectedly felled by – of all things – mumps! I therefore went to Southampton at the end of October when the weather was, in fact, rather better than it had been throughout August. It was a bright sunny day, ideal for cricket, but the only activity on the grass was the heavy mower roaring around the outfield while Tony Smetham, the ground maintenance manager, worked away on the 'scarifier', making holes in the ground. It is amazing how much grass clipping you produce when you mow a cricket field. There were two skips full of the stuff. The outfield had been cut very low but the square was growing lush and green – a curious reversal of what it looks like in summer.

Matthew Engel, the *Guardian*'s cricket writer, says Hampshire are a running certainty for the Diabolical Press Box award but otherwise praises Southampton for being the most typical of the county grounds. 'Not too posh like the Test grounds,' he says, 'not too red-brick and depressing like some of the Midland grounds, not too obviously – and self-consciously – pretty, like Worcester or the Kent grounds, and certainly not too drearily run down, like Bristol.' So what does it have to offer? 'Middlingness,' suggests Engel. Ho Hum!

Mr James, an avuncular figure in a Royal Artillery tie, met me at the station. He says there are two bus routes which pass reasonably close to the ground, but it is about a mile from the City Centre and the luminous yellow AA signs which are up all summer had been removed. You can gauge the sort of neighbourhood it is in from the proximity of the Bannister Park Bowling Club. On that side of the ground behind the pavilion and grandstand, white and Edwardian in style, with a new red roof, there are substantial Victorian villas. John Arlott says of the pavilion: 'With its bright red tiles and brickwork, white woodwork, and open to the air, in perpetual optimistic expectation of sunshine, it is – or is it merely the nostalgia makes it seem so? – a generous, essentially summer place.' Nostalgic, possibly, but not far off the mark. And there are only three executive boxes in the top of the building. Very unobtrusive too.

There used to be a greyhound and speedway track here, but that has vanished, and along one side of the ground are some modern maisonettes with huge plate glass windows affording one of the best free views in modern county cricket. Along another is what looks like a modern council estate. Apart from the pavilion area the stands are exceedingly utilitarian. The plastic bucket seat has not yet come to Southampton. The stands are little more than scaffolding with wooden benches. Mr James says it's a grand place when it's full. But it has to be admitted that it is a bit dull when it is empty. The most amusing building is the old mock-Tudor home team dressing-room. The least amusing is the office block, opened by H. S. Altham in 1956 – ugly without and cramped within.

The most spectacular new development has been the squash and social centre near the main entrance, built at a cost of £300,000 in an attempt, as Mark Nicholas says, 'to redress the wrong – and red – side of the county's balance sheet.' Mr James was keen to point out that it was the 'County Cricket Club Squash and Social Centre' and very much part of the club – not a sort of interloper. Indeed he was adamant all the time that the Hampshire CCC was a private members' club. It is a point not always emphasised elsewhere.

The squash and social centre is not a thing of great beauty but it is very well appointed. There are four squash courts, two cricket nets, a gym and jacuzzi, restaurant, bar, dining-rooms and a disco exercise studio 'incorporating California Workout, Disco Exercise Classes, Aerobics and Fitness Programmes'. They even boast 'Beauty Treatments and Health Advice available for both members and non-members'. I am not sure what 'Lordship' Tennyson would have made of that.

His photograph, together with that of all the other Hampshire captains, is on the stairs. He looks enormous and the epitome of pugnaciousness. A group of dark-suited executive lunchers passed by while I was there and one of them remarked, blasphemously, 'Funny how once their career is over, they just sort of vanish.' Vanish indeed. One former captain, Ronnie Aird, is now joint patron of the club with Lord Denning, while another, Cecil Paris, is the club's president. Lord Tennyson, grandson of the laureate, was captain from 1919 to 1933, which means that he must presumably have captained the side which beat Nottingham on 23 May 1930 and produced the most eccentric sight of the entire Nottinghamshire side fielding in lounge suits, with Barrett and Voce in overcoats and several men in hats. At the beginning of the last day Hampshire only needed a single run to win with five wickets standing. Notts couldn't be bothered to get changed. A. W. Carr bowled and had the winning runs struck off his second ball to Kennedy. The photograph is proudly displayed outside the Desmond Eagar Room.

The prominence given to Eagar's name around the Southampton ground is scarcely surprising, because for years he was the most significant cricketing figure in the county. His batting average was only just over 21, and his bowling average 62, but he was captain from 1946 to 1957, combining the captaincy with the role of secretary and continuing as secretary until his early death in 1977. It was he, more than anyone, who was responsible for building the side that won Hampshire's first ever championship in 1961.

There is a jolly montage of photographs of that famous occasion, which happened down the road in Bournemouth (now technically in Dorset). The rather fuzzy black-and-white pictures show action and celebration, in both of which activities Ingleby-Mackenzie, a captain in the Tennyson mould, is taking part and looking immensely cheerful. The photographer credited with capturing these moments is one E. P. Eagar, Desmond's son, and now the most successful cricket photographer on the circuit. He has improved as a photographer since then.

'This is a story I have been waiting fifteen years to write,' said 'Nomad' in the *Southern Evening Echo*, while *The Times* described them as 'the heirs of Hambledon' and those ancient Hampshire heroes who beat everyone in sight 'on Broadhalfpenny Down so long ago'. The inimitable Swanton wrote: 'It is a slight exaggeration to imagine the Hampshire dressing-room as a focus for trainers and tipsters with private wires to Newmarket and Burlington Street. At the same time

Ingleby-Mackenzie rules with a light touch and plays cricket with a smile that is reflected in his team. This is not the worst reason why Hampshire will be hailed as the welcome and popular champions of 1961.'

It is sometimes said that nothing very momentous ever happened on the county ground here, and yet it has not all been 'middlingness'. In the administration block they preserve the scorecard of the 1952 game when they got Kent out for 32 and 91 and Shackleton took twelve for 67 and Cannings eight for 55. John Arlott recalls the day Bradman went to his thousand runs in May with a four off a Jack Newman full-toss. In 1912 the county beat the Australians here by eight wickets, thanks largely to Mead's 160 and Kennedy's eleven wickets. No other county beat the Australians till Surrey in 1956. But the best day ever must have been in 1928, when the West Indies came to Southampton. Constantine, bowling very fast, took the first four for 24, and at 86 for five 'Lordship' came in. He and Newman proceeded to put on 313 and Tennyson made 217 in four hours with a six and 27 fours. Oddly enough the sixth wicket has been the most prolific in Hampshire records. At the top of the stairs by the secretary's office is the silk scorecard from 1899 when Captain Wynyard and Major Poore put on 411 against Somerset. There is still a handsome silver cup inscribed with Major Poore's name. It sits in a corner cupboard in the secretary's office looking unwanted.

That was at Taunton, though, and it is true that too many of the great Hampshire achievements have been away from home. Witness

the scorecard of 'A match is never lost until it is won' presented by 'Friends in Winchester'. It was June 1922. Warwickshire made 223 and bowled out Hampshire for 15. When Hampshire followed on they made 521 and then got their hosts all out for 158. Funny old game!

At times it has been a harsh one, too. The most disconcerting document at Southampton is Remnant's contract. Remnant played from 1918 to 1922 and his piece of paper is headed 'Regulations and Remuneration as to staff'. It begins by saying that not more than twenty-five shillings should be paid to any man taken on as a first-class professional. It then stipulates the hours – ten to seven with an hour and a half for dinner, but 'to be entitled to a full day's pay each professional must sign the book kept for that purpose ... by ten a.m. and before or after dinner.' Another section says that 'cards and gambling are strictly prohibited'. Bowlers not playing on match days are 'expected to make themselves useful in any manner required'. And although it was accepted that professionals could seek employment during the winter, they were not allowed to do so without the sanction of the committee. You have to be very careful talking about the 'good old days' when it comes to cricket – here or anywhere else.

Mr Secretary James, commonly known as 'Jimmy', is a Cheshire man who spent many years in East Africa, where he did a lot of umpiring. He thinks they are lucky in the south of England. The cricket crowds are still well behaved, appreciative and polite. The whole atmosphere is very friendly. 'We have a small police presence at Sunday league matches. And if there's the slightest trouble we immediately close the bars. And we throw them out for obscene language.' The team is young and promising and if the ground is a bit middling he is happy enough. With temporary stands it can accommodate just over six thousand. 'But,' he says, 'I'd rather have six thousand happy than six and a half unhappy.'

I think this probably sums up the Hampshire philosophy rather well. They have always tended to play cavalier cricket, from Tennyson's time through to Ingleby-Mackenzie's, and on to that of Pocock and Nicholas. It wasn't all that easy to conjure up that summery picture Arlott evokes as I scuffed through the fallen brown leaves behind the pavilion or contemplated the old bell of the liner *Athlone Castle* which hangs in front of it. But I could see that it was a pleasant place. I asked Mr James if he would be back in retirement and he muttered irascibly that, despite the fine view from his office window, he was lucky if he got a chance to see twenty minutes of a game all day. But next year, he said, with a touch of defiance, he'd be back with his wife and some haversack rations and a couple of deck chairs and he'd sit on the opposite side of the ground and take the greatest possible pleasure in doing nothing whatever but watch the cricket. He is, he claims, never going to sit on a committee ever again.

I sense that Lord Tennyson would approve the sentiment.

TRANTRIDGE HARDY

'Always my favourite village'

There is no longer a railway station at Trantridge Hardy. For seventy-three years it was connected to Sherborne via a branch line of the old Dorset and Wiltshire light railway, which meandered across those counties from Lyme Regis in the south-west to Bath in the north. It was hopelessly uneconomic and, inevitably, fell to the Beeching axe. Nowadays the only way to the village is the B748 which used to run straight down the High Street but now bypasses it half a mile to the south.

Trantridge Hardy has always been my favourite village because once, when I was fifteen, staying with my schoolmate Lorimer, I played for them against Nether Mynton. There was an outbreak of Asian flu or swine fever or something equally exotic, and two of the Trantridge men couldn't play so Lorimer and I were drafted. I batted at number ten and made three not out but, fielding at square leg, I caught a blinding catch off their star batsman just as he seemed to be set on a match-winning innings. It was pure self-defence: a full-blooded sweep off the meat of the bat, head height. If I hadn't got my hands to it, I'd have been decapitated. The Nether Mynton innings fell apart after that and we won by eleven runs. That evening in The Bat and Ball I first tasted Veuve Clicquot champagne.

It has hardly changed since then. In fact it must be much the same as it was a hundred or even two hundred years ago. There is something to be said for Beeching and the bypass: they have kept the ravages of the twentieth century at bay. There are no modern houses, no industry, not even a Chinese take-away. The nearest thing to a punk is Lorimer's fifteen-year-old daughter, who does have pierced ears but would pass as a conventional Sloane on the King's Road.

For reasons of sentiment I chose the day of the Nether Mynton match for my visit and I was rewarded by one of the few really beautiful days of the summer. By eleven o'clock, when I pulled up at the Old Rectory, where Lorimer still lives, it was over seventy and rising. The sky was a very pale blue and quite cloudless. There was the faintest suspicion of a breeze – a zephyr if you were in a poetic frame of mind – and the countryside had that wonderful fresh lime green quality which you only get in early summer.

'You're opening,' said Lorimer, who runs the family solicitors in Beaminster now that his father's dead. Lorimer is captain of Trantridge Hardy – another inheritance from his father who was still playing the summer before he died. Still quite a sprightly wicket-keeper, according to Lorimer, even at sixty-four. 'Only joking,' he added, laughing at my obvious dismay, 'We're at full strength, I'm happy to say. Which is more than we were at Nether Mynton in May. We shouldn't have played really. Huge puddle at one end and they had a demon leg spinner who found the deepest spot three times out of four. You needed windscreen wipers to play him. We were all out for 32.

It's only a couple of hundred yards from the Rectory to the ground, so we walked down there, Lorimer carrying his old cricket bag, still the same one he had at school. It has holes in it now and the leather corners are all worn away, but I did very much admire the label which said 'S.S. *CARINTHIA*. Not required on voyage.' Also Lorimer's bat, an antique Gunn and Moore, almost black from countless seasons of linseed oil, and bound and rebound so that it looked like a very old war wound.

I suppose there are prettier grounds in England, but I've not seen one. What's more it's even better since the bypass as there is practically no traffic along the High Street, which forms the boundary at the Bat and Ball end. At the other end the pavilion is raised above the field on a grass platform about ten foot up. Players enter the fray down steps cut in the slope. The pavilion itself is white clapboard with a newly thatched roof and a little plaque saying '1864. H.M.M.'. This refers to Sir Humphrey Manderson, fourteenth baronet, who caused the building to be erected. His great-great-great-grandson – give or take a generation – was Trantridge's fastest bowler. Just missed his blue at Cambridge. His partner, marginally slower but steadier, was Ralph Bodger who, under the Youth Opportunities Scheme, had helped his father thatch the pavilion.

The hills stretch away behind the pavilion – wooded round the edge, bare on top, like a tonsure, which is appropriate since the old pilgrim's track leads to the home of the Franciscan Friars at Batcombe. The hills make a perfect backdrop.

If the bowling is from the pavilion end then the midwicket boundary is the church side of the ground. The Manderson alms-houses extend neatly from long-on to deep square leg. Then there is a yew hedge, a short stretch of churchyard, and finally, beyond where a rather fine long-leg would stand, there is the fourteenth-century church of St Anselm, laid on tenth-century foundations with its famous and uniquely leaning eighteenth-century spire. Pevsner was ecstatic about the church, especially the Manderson tombs.

Trantridge Manor lies about five hundred yards over cover point. In fact the story is that Learie Constantine drove a ball into the ha-ha one day in the twenties when Sir Alfred Manderson, young Manderson's grandfather, invited him down to join Colonel ffrench-Drake's eleven for the final day of the Trantridge Cricket Week. The Manor is essentially Tudor but has been knocked about a bit by Cromwell and others, then 'improved', mainly by the Victorians. It's a bit chaotic, but fun. For the Nether Mynton match the traditional 'Manderson Marquee', complete with bunting, had been dutifully pitched the night before.

Lorimer and I sauntered into the pavilion and he introduced me to one or two of the players: Desmond Gauvinier, the local vet, a cousin of the famous Tillingfold players, Peter and Paul; the publican from the Bat and Ball, Len Sprott; Mr Midge, the butcher; the Reverend Peter Chamberlain, vicar of Trantridge Hardy and also of Trantridge D'Urberville and Trantridge St Thomas, the neighbouring villages; a writer called Southcott; and a jovial fat man who seemed to answer to the name of 'Jingle'. (I gathered he was in advertising.)

The pavilion had an inimitable smell that took me back a quarter of a century: a compound of linseed oil and mothball and mown grass. I was pleased to see that the village's main cricketing heirloom was still in its glass case by the door of the home dressing-room. 'Dr W. G. Grace's pad,' said the brass plaque. 'This pad was worn by "W.G."' on the occasion of his visit to Trantridge Hardy on May 17th 1874'. It was true. I had seen the scorebook which showed, preposterously, that the Doctor had been bowled by Squire Manderson for a duck. He had obviously been peeved about this because when Trantridge batted he took seven wickets for only four – including the squire – caught and bowled for two.

We sat and chatted for a while and then the Nether Mynton team coach arrived and I drifted away from the players and found a deck-chair under the old oak outside the saloon bar of the Bat and Ball. The game started a few minutes after noon and a few minutes after that I wandered into the bar and bought a pint of 'Old Parsnip' from Len Sprott's extremely attractive daughter. Trantridge had won the toss and elected to bat. Gauvinier was at number one, an elegant left-hander in an I Zingari cap, partnered by young Manderson, bare-headed and impetuous, who cut his first ball from the Nether Mynton fast bowler for four, then miscued a hook off the next and was very nearly caught by square leg running backwards, but the sun got in his eyes and he fell over and the ball trickled over the boundary for four. Gauvinier came down the wicket and had a quiet word with Manderson, telling him, I presumed, not to be quite so hasty. I sipped my Old Parsnip, which is good beer, real as anything, and I thought of England.

Village cricket has been dignified with its own national competition sponsored by Samuel Whitbread, the brewers, who make good beer though nothing as delicious as Old Parsnip. They have their final at Lord's, which is a splendid accolade for the grass roots game and yet not entirely appropriate. I tried to envisage Trantridge Hardy and Nether Mynton battling it out in that cavernous arena before empty stands, and shuddered slightly. Village cricket belongs, I decided, on village greens. It is played by genuine amateurs for genuine fun. Young Manderson executed a definitive Surrey cut and thundered down the wicket with a bellow of 'Come two!', thus confirming my thought.

'Here with a Pint of Beer beneath the Bough,' I mused, and wandered over to chat up Old Fred, the scorer whom I had recognised

192

earlier. He was a small, nut-brown man who worked for the council; mainly as a hedge trimmer. He had scored for the village for fifty years and had done so the day I played against Nether Mynton. Not that he recognised me, though when I introduced myself he said at once:

'Well I'll be dashed! You were the young lad that caught Major Trumpington in fifty-nine.'

'Yes,' I said, modestly.

'Major Trumpington didn't like that,' said Old Fred, 'He didn't like that a bit.'

I watched for a moment over his shoulder, marvelling at the neatness and precision of the dots and numbers as he recorded the progress of the innings; also at the immaculate copperplate as the inevitable happened and he had to write 'stumped Basset bowled Kerridge' against Manderson's name. Manderson had made 32, mainly in boundaries. He had been trying to heave the ball, à la Constantine, into the ha-ha, but played an air-shot half-way down the wicket and could not regain his ground.

We lunched at 1.30 in the tent. There were trestle tables and ham salad or pork pie and salad, and fruit salad and farmhouse cheddar. Wives and girlfriends joined in, and the umpires and scorers too. Charles Lorimer had to jump up and shoo away someone's dog which strayed on to the field of play and cocked its leg against the wicket. His father told the Nether Mynton captain about my catch. Danvers and Perkins, both local farmers, talked about subsidies and butter mountains. The vicar defended the Bishop of Durham not very wholeheartedly. Gauvinier, the vet, attacked James Herriot.

I dozed off for a moment or two afterwards back in the deck chair under the tree. It was hot, and the batting had slowed after Manderson's first brave onslaught. The Old Parsnip made me drowsy. That and the soporific perfection of the day.

At tea Trantridge were 182 all out. Nether Mynton ten for one. Manderson took the wicket with a fast full-toss.

Tea was also served in the tent. There were cup-cakes and egg sandwiches and cucumber sandwiches and marmite sandwiches and tarts. The tea came from an old urn, and was hot and weak and milky and sweet. Old Fred sat with me and told me how he had seen Hobbs and Sutcliffe one year at the Oval and how there had never been a batsman as pretty as Woolley or as inexorable as Hutton but that if old Patridge the squire's gamekeeper who bowled off-spin for Trantridge for nigh on thirty years had been a Surrey or a Yorkshire man he'd have played for England, but seeing as how Dorset didn't have a first-class team and how the squire was a hard master – hard but fair, mind – and Patridge having lost the tip of his index finger at Ypres, besides which and one thing and another and it hadn't been the same since they started covering wickets and this one-day stuff wasn't what you'd call cricket now was it, not really, but you had to hand it to that Geoffrey Boycott, know what I mean, I mean say what you like but . . . .

And there was honey from the parson's bees.

Then I went back to the deck chair and I thought of England again and Nether Mynton got to 179 for nine and Lorimer brought on Mr Midge, the butcher, who bowled very slow leg breaks. The Nether Mynton number eleven hit the first one for a scampered three to the long leg boundary, then with the scores level, the other batsman, a strong, cocky estate agent, went for glory, got a top edge and was beautifully caught by Lorimer's son, Charles.

'Funny old game,' said Lorimer, over a pint in the Bat and Ball, 'but a fair result.'

'Very fair result,' said the Nether Mynton captain.

'Dream catch,' said Gauvinier.

'Dream match,' I said, savouring another pint of Old Parsnip. A perfect game in a perfect village on a perfect day. The apotheosis of cricket at its most bucolic, least pretentious and most blissfully elusive. If Trantridge Hardy and its pitch and its team didn't exist, you would have to invent them.

LORD'S

*'Ancient bats
and balls . . .
ancient members
perched on chairs
and tables'*

Cricket grounds are like seaside resorts. They come alive in summer with the sunshine and the deck chairs and the bunting and the bands, but like seaside resorts I find them oddly appealing out of season when they are empty and windswept. I see that this is perverse, but there is something romantic about the melancholy of deserted stands, the odd piece of flapping canvas, sea-gulls standing on the square, dejected but undisturbed.

One chill day in winter I came in to Lord's for a game of Real Tennis. They were rebuilding the squash courts and changing-rooms, so for once the tennis players, usually consigned to a rather poor relation status behind the pavilion, were allowed to change in the Middlesex and England dressing-room. The dressing-room felt as if it had been untouched since about 1947 and the days of the Compton-Edrich ascendancy and, perversely, that too gave it a strange romance. When it is titivated, as it presumably will be, it will become much harder to think of those Brylcreem heroes actually padding up in that very room. It had snowed during the night and I was playing early. The whole of the ground was covered in white and there wasn't a footmark on it. I have never seen Lord's looking better.

Even in season there is something about being at Lord's on a very quiet day. One day early in summer I was walking towards the Nursery End when MCC were playing the MCC professionals. I had vaguely assumed that MCC would be represented exclusively by retired majors in Eaton Rambler sweaters. I paused. The scoreboard said that MCC's opening bat was 58 not out. He looked oddly familiar and not a bit like an Old Etonian major. It was Geoffrey Boycott. I bought a scorecard and settled down. Seconds later there was a bowling change. The captain was bringing himself on. 'Mr D's bowling', said a knowledgeable voice, and sure enough it was the tall thin figure of the Lord's coach. He beat him once too, going for the sweep, hit him on the front pad. Not out, of course, but a moment to savour. G. Boycott, Yorkshire and England, versus D. Wilson, Yorkshire and England. I suppose there might have been thirty of us in the ground. Better that, oddly enough, than thirty thousand.

The inescapable Cardus seems to have had a similar notion, though not quite so extreme. 'A hundred times,' he wrote in his autobiography, 'I have walked down the St John's Wood Road on a quiet morning – that's the proper way to enjoy Lord's: choose a match of no importance, for preference one for which the fixture card promises "a band if possible". I have gone a hundred times into the Long Room out of the hot sun and never have I not felt that this is a good place to be in; and if the English simply had to make cricket a national

198

institution and a passion and a pride, this was the way to do it.' I particularly like 'a band if possible'! Lord's, of all grounds, should always have a band.

Playing Real Tennis at Lord's – a new recreation in danger of becoming obsessive – I've seen the place often out of season and also learned something about that curious extramural activity which takes place behind the pavilion (no, not THAT sort of activity). Real Tennis seems to come naturally to cricketers, at least to batsmen. Douglas Jardine was the Oxford number one; F. R. Brown was good; Colin Cowdrey and Ted Dexter especially so. 'The stroke is like a cover drive,' says Henry Johns, leaning elegantly into a textbook batless demonstration in the pro shop. 'Batsmen find it easier than bowlers because they can read the spin and follow the flight.' Norman Cowans, who spent a winter as a young pro, impressed everyone with his cheerfulness and his dedication but it was obvious that he was never going to be one of the world's great tennis players.

Mr Johns is the doyen of tennis and a keen observer of the cricketing scene as well. Years ago he had a flat overlooking the ground. From it he could see the queues forming the night before the Australian Test match and he would watch early on the morning of the first day as MCC's secretary Colonel Rait Kerr (who played Real Rennis for the club) came out and made a ritual presentation of two free tickets to the people at the very head of the queue. There were buskers to entertain the queue and vendors hawking food and drink. On the morning of the Eton and Harrow match Henry could see the flower sellers turning up at six and dyeing their carnations in the traditional light blue of Eton. (It was, as Etonians are always pointing out, Eton blue long before being appropriated by Cambridge.) Harrow wore dark blue carnations, and the nobbier supporters of both schools brought horse-drawn carriages which they parked at the Nursery End, where they picnicked on the grass.

The final of the Gold Racquet was moved from Oxford and Cambridge to Eton and Harrow at Douglas Jardine's insistence (he was involved in both the Varsity match and the tennis final) and drew capacity crowds. Harold Macmillan always came; ladies were not allowed on the closely packed benches in the dedans but watched from the galleries high above the court. One year, just as Henry Johns was about to start the game, a lady dropped her handbag which burst open on the penthouse scattering its contents, including powder, all over the court. Henry had to postpone the tennis and get a step ladder to retrieve the bag. Even when the Gold Racquet was not being played it was customary for the Etonians and Harrovians to pause from their gentle amble round the ground and meet for a brief chat in the court. All changed now, however. In the shires, especially the north, men will mutter caustically about the feudal aristocratic traditions of Lord's and say that the Eton and Harrow match is the high point of the year for the MCC committee, but it's not true. The game nowadays *is* an anachronism and if the truth be told should really go the way of all those other anachronisms which were banished from cricket HQ years ago – Beaumont and Oratory, Clifton and Tonbridge. Yet they like to put on *one* public school match, and nowadays there are Lord's games for representative sides of state schoolboys too.

Many of the Real Tennis professionals around the country are men who came to the Lord's court from 'the cricket side' and were taught the game by Henry Johns: David Johnson at Queen's (he won the bat for most promising young batsman three years running); Brian Church at Cambridge; Peter Dawes at Hayling Island. The present chief pro, David Cull, came over twenty-five years ago as a young medium-pacer and was quickly transformed by the coach Bill Watkin into an off-spinner.

'I gave it a season,' he says, 'then I came over one day for a game of squash with the lads.' He had scarcely heard of squash, let alone played it, but he thought it was fun and stayed through the winter as the most junior of four pros on the tennis side. He was supposed to go back to cricket next summer but stayed on behind the pavilion. He never told Gus Farley, the ground superintendent in charge of the boys, and got a rollicking from him.

He was so small then that he could barely see over the net. Indeed the assistant secretary of MCC, S. C. 'Billy' Griffith, had been seriously concerned about whether he could stand up to the workload. 'These boys now have it so easy' is David Cull's verdict on the modern generation. 'We had to get here at eight in the morning and sweep the whole ground. Then help the fellows with the roller. On match days you sold scorecards – you got a farthing for each one. Another thing I did was work in the scorebox. That was my bunce.

'Crumbs, I loved it though. I remember when I first came here and I was the only boy without a bat and pads. They said get changed and I got changed and they said, "Where's your bat and pads?" and I said, "I'm a bowler." I mean I thought at Lord's they'd provide all the gear. But my mother, she was so proud of me she found the money and got me the bat and pads.'

They run your bath for you at Lord's, and Henry Johns and David Cull call their members 'Sir' and 'Mister'. Nothing as familiar as a christian name would ever pass their lips, and while at first I found this oppressive I got used to it after a while. They maintain that they have just as much fun with their members and know them as well as the pro's do at places where they appear to be more egalitarian. I was reminded of something which Major Ronnie Ferguson once told me about his attitude to Prince Phillip when he captained him at polo. 'You said exactly the same to him as to anyone else,' he said. 'You just put "sir" on the end.'

David Cull says, 'I've never ever entertained the thought of leaving.

It's the atmosphere ... the friendliness. .... You've still got your characters, and it's still the same, because everyone who works here, they love it. It's a great place.'

Sadly, however, his appetite for cricket seems to have diminished. 'I used to watch from the pavilion,' he says, 'especially when Jack Robertson was batting. I remember Compton and Edrich and Warr and Moss. But nowadays half the time I couldn't tell you who was playing. It was buzzing there around that time, but somehow it doesn't buzz any longer.'

It was about that time that I first came to Lord's. The family caught the train from Gerrards Cross to Marylebone and the tube from there to St John's Wood. We sat in the Mound or somewhere near the Old Tavern and the Clock Tower restaurant. Certainly I remember Robertson well – rather upright, cap somewhat stiff. I saw Compton's last appearance and was quite impressed by the speed of Warr and Moss, though they were nothing like Statham. I remember Statham zapping through three Middlesex or maybe MCC wickets for practically nothing. There was a buzz then all right. I got Denis Compton's autograph, but missed out on David Lean who was chatting to him at the time. I had never heard of Lean then and was ticked off by an onlooker who thought David Lean a much more substantial figure than Compton. I would still rather have Compton's autograph than Lean's. I waylaid the Bedsers once and thought them horribly snubbing and offhand. Eric signed, but Alec didn't. I have been prejudiced against him ever since, though, to be fair, he was much nicer and more relaxed the other day when he came in to the tennis changing-room to weigh himself on the jockey's scales. He seemed quite pleased with the result.

For me Lord's is the best of all cricket grounds because it was the first. I have been going there for over thirty years and I have been a member of MCC for more than a decade. I think the pavilion is one of the world's most evocative buildings. It suggests elegance and escape and on big match days it and the whole ground still have a buzz for me. I love watching a great cricketer, past or present, making a stately progress during the lunch or tea interval. During the last of the England–Australia one-day matches I saw Colin Cowdrey, nut-brown and beaming, walking very slowly along the tarmac behind the pavilion and acknowledging greeting and reverence. And you could sense the crowd all thinking, 'Ah, Cowdrey ... if only he were playing.'

As it was, Gooch and Gower made hundreds, and although they were only playing for the plate, England thumped Australia. I was in the Long Room when Gower came in, bat raised high and punching the air with his fist. It was the end of an appalling run of low scores, and the members seemed as relieved by the century as the England captain himself. Often I have seen players come through the Long Room staring moodily at the floor or the ceiling, apparently determined to ignore the members. Too often there seems an unbridgeable gulf between the young professionals earning their living and the clubbable members taking time off to be spectators.

That day the place was so packed that the only place I could find was on the bridge between the pavilion and Q Stand. A lot of members aren't really aware of this, because you have to go down a private-looking passage past the England dressing-room to get to it. The view is excellent, and that day it was full of serious and gossipy cricketers who were happy to fill me in on the proceedings so far, and particularly gleeful in describing how cross Phil Edmonds had been at being left out and how he had come straight out of the dressing-room looking like thunder and made a series of phone calls. I would have played him myself because, like Randall, he is always doing something, even if it's only chatting up the umpires.

'I know you from somewhere,' said the member on my left suddenly. 'Where do you play your cricket?'

I said I hadn't played cricket since my golden duck, opening the innings against Great Tew in 1965. He didn't believe me.

'I know,' he said. 'You play for the Nomads. That's it. You're a Nomad.'

And try as I might, I could do nothing to shake this belief.

1985 was a surprisingly good Lord's summer because, despite the pervading damp, the sun shone on St John's Wood when it mattered. The Test was won by Australia by four wickets, a victory memorable chiefly for an innings of 196 from Border and for the fact that it was started on time. (Everybody was full of stories about how they had walked on to the outfield and found water coming over their insteps. Somehow the ground staff, working all through the night, managed to dry it out.) There was sun for the one-day Texaco which England won by eight wickets; sun for the Benson and Hedges final; and sun for the NatWest.

I quite enjoyed the Benson and Hedges, though it has never been my favourite final. There always seem to be more rowdies than usual, perhaps because the game is played so emphatically outside the soccer season. I always feel the crowd is nearer to a soccer one than on any other cricket occasion. More booze, more mindless shouting. Not that it was too bad this time, though for the first time in my life I was heckled under the Grandstand for wearing an MCC tie.

In this one Leicester beat Essex by five wickets with three overs to spare. It sounds easy, but it wasn't until a fine sixth-wicket stand between Willey and the sprightly Garnham, a young wicket-keeper who soon afterwards announced a premature retirement, that the thing was settled. They made an unbeaten eighty together and got them in twelve overs.

The NatWest final was more exciting, carrying on into the murk of a September evening with Nottingham almost snatching an unlikely win over Essex. They were chasing 280, and got hopelessly behind the clock. Randall, at his most chirpy, almost pulled them back, but they still needed 18 off the last over. Despite the most defensive field imaginable he somehow took sixteen runs off Pringle's first five balls, only to hole out off the sixth. There is nothing like being part of a Lord's crowd on occasions like that.

Of course it is not everyone's cup of tea. 'It's not Wembley,' remarked Jack Bailey, MCC's secretary, gazing across at the builders working on the new Mound Stand (courtesy of J. Paul Getty). But a lot of people think it *is* cricket's Wembley and find it hard to reconcile the notion with the fact that MCC is a private club with a twenty-year waiting list. It seems rather strange to me too, but I find that I can accept the idea. But then, enjoying the privileges of membership, I would, wouldn't I? On the other hand all county cricket clubs are private members' clubs, it's just that they don't have the good fortune, like MCC, of being over-subscribed. You can hardly blame MCC for being desirable. And isn't it better to have a club owned by several thousand members, none of them necessarily very rich, than a club owned by one millionaire and dictated to by a board of directors? Give me MCC and Lord's rather than any soccer club in the League. Yet how often do you hear about Old Trafford or White Hart Lane being 'undemocratic'?

In fact non-members have freer access at Lord's than many county grounds. At Headingley and Northampton, to pick two at random, you are not allowed to walk right round the ground. But at Lord's you can watch the teams limbering up in the nets at the Nursery End – there were huge crowds contemplating the Australians in their incongruous yellow-and-green tracksuits. And you can walk under the

Grandstand and behind the pavilion, gawping as you go. The new Mound Stand, financed by Getty, has been designed with a special arched walk-way to maintain this principle. It's just the pavilion which is a clubhouse. Only members are allowed in the pavilion, to snooze in the reading room, sit in one of the high chairs in the Long Room, or sample the sea food in the restaurant at the top.

You could write a book about Lord's. Geoffrey Moorhouse did. Moorhouse is a Lancashire lad and not a natural MCC ally, but the book is scrupulously fair and meticulous, and by and large the club and ground emerge with credit. 'If that's the worst anyone can write about us then we're not doing too badly' was one mainstream MCC verdict I heard. For the 1987 bicentenary MCC has commissioned Tony Lewis, a former captain of Cambridge, England and Glamorgan as well as the *Sunday Telegraph* cricket man. (Moorhouse used to write for the *Manchester Guardian*.) Lewis is a more obvious choice but, as it turned out, the Moorhouse book was a wonderful piece of public relations. You expect an encomium from a fancy hat like Lewis. Not from a cloth cap like Moorhouse.

Lord's does change, but it changes with measured tread. There will, for instance, be bucket seats in the new Mound Stand but not elsewhere. At least not yet. When I asked Jack Bailey about them he said that there was something to be said for bench seating. On a quiet day you could put your feet up, spread out, have room for the sandwiches and the scorebooks. And you can always hire a cushion if you have a sensitive backside. There will be 'improvements' at Lord's but not much in the way of dramatic change. 'It's like buying a new pair of shoes,' says Bailey. 'The minute you've got them that serviceable old suit suddenly starts to look a bit shabby and you feel you have to get a new one.' So the minute the new Mound Stand is finished people will turn their attentions to the newly evident tattiness of the Grandstand and the Nursery stands.

If you want chapter and verse about Lord's you must refer to Moorhouse. Moorhouse has a map. And several pages devoted exclusively to Gubby Allen. And the precise number of pints consumed on Cup Final days.

For me, Lord's has a special and inimitable atmosphere; a compound of personal memory and corporate nostalgia; of anachronistic hierarchies and deferences and rules; of the best cricket I ever watch; of a sense of occasion no matter if the ground is packed full of noisy partisans or if only a single slow handclap echoes round the stands. There is something about the place which is as timeless as a cathedral or a village green, and there is far more to it than cricket.

'Inside the W. G. Grace gates,' wrote Robertson-Glasgow, 'I saw the same spectator whom I always see on my first day at Lord's. He was waiting for his brother; who is always late. And there was the field itself. How green, after the huge, glaring, yellowy arenas of Australia.

'But I missed the member with his telescope which he balances on the front rail of the pavilion, bending low to fix his eye on the footwork of the batsmen and the very texture of the pitch. He will surely arrive, when the sun is stronger, and he has finished cataloguing the ships at sea, or the stars in the May sky. He will, of course, bring his field glasses as well, for double verification.

'In the afternoon sun the Tavern grew more argumentative. On the grassy plot behind the Rover stand, one man sat with his back to the match, achieving that elusive triumph of thinking of absolutely nothing at all. Another spectator lay fast asleep, content with the mere fact of cricket and his own absence from the roar of traffic, from invoices, or the blare of his neighbour's radio. He would wake in an hour or so, and tell them all wrong, all about the cricket, when he reached home.'

The timeless continuity of Lord's withstands all its changes. I've been going there so long that I feel it is always the same even when – in detail – it manifestly isn't. I recognise the gatemen these days, and I look out for Henry Johns and David Cull standing in those ducky new white track-suits the tennis players now affect, guarding their territory behind the pavilion. I know where to look for Jonners and Blowers and the rest of the BBC commentary team as they scale the steps to their turret high above the play. I hope to see journalists like Mark Boxer, the editor of the *Tatler*, or Godfrey Smith of the *Sunday Times* or Michael Davie of the *Observer*; or the novelist Simon Raven; or the poet P. J. Kavanagh; or David Webb Carter, the Brigadier from Belize. I remember days with family and friends; hundreds from Gooch and from Gower; pyrotechnics from Dexter and Richards and Botham; Brearley's captaincy; Titmus's spin; and Edmonds and Emburey; and Peter Parfitt and Don Bennett. I like to walk slowly round the ground, moving from rowdiness in the claustrophobic dark under the Grandstand to a murmur in the pavilion balcony and euphoric excess at trestle tables in the old arbours at the Nursery End. I always pause before that wonderful portrait of the founders of I Zingari and walk slowly through the Long Room, enjoying the ancient bats and balls in glass cases and the ancient members perched on chairs and tables.

It's elusive, the true character of cricket, and you can find aspects of it everywhere the game is played and watched, but nowhere more than here at Lord's, headquarters of the game, where they have been playing for almost two hundred years and are still going strong.